BALANCED RIDING

BALANCED RIDING

A Way to Find the Correct Seat

by

Pegotty Henriques

To Julia, my daughter, whose own interest as a very young rider drew me into dressage; for the fun we had together when she rode, and for the fun we have together now.

© Text and illustrations Pegotty Henriques 1987

First published in the United States 1987 by
Half Halt Press, Box 3512, Gaithersburg, Maryland 20878

Designed by Neil Clitheroe.

Library of Congress Cataloging-in-Publication Data

Henriques, Pegotty.
  Balanced riding.
  1. Horsemanship. I. Title.
SF309.H445 1987   61798.2   87-17730

ISBN 0-939481-01-4

Printed in Great Britain.

CONTENTS

	INTRODUCTION	6
1	WHY DOES THE CORRECT POSITION MATTER?	7
2	THE PATH TO LEARNING	10
3	THE RIDER'S PHYSIQUE	14
4	THE RIDER'S SENSES	21
5	THE SADDLE: ITS IMPORTANCE AND INFLUENCE	26
6	THE CORRECT POSITION AT THE HALT	32
7	THE WALK	40
8	THE TROT	43
9	THE CANTER	51
10	FUNDAMENTAL PROBLEMS	56
11	INTRODUCTION TO THE APPLICATION OF THE AIDS	61
12	THE LEG POSITION	64
13	THE REIN AIDS	68
14	THE SEAT, BACK AND WEIGHT AIDS	77
15	EXERCISES FOR THE RIDER	83
16	LUNGEING THE RIDER	91
17	RIDER POSITION FAULTS	95
	FAULTS RELATED TO BALANCE	96
18	FAULTS RELATED TO CROOKEDNESS	109
19	FAULTS CAUSED BY TENSION	121
20	FAULTS CAUSED BY LOOSENESS	142
21	WHEN THE BRAIN GETS IN THE WAY	153
	INDEX	155

INTRODUCTION

For many years I have struggled with my own very faulty position. I am also well aware of my own mental and physical inadequacies, and would dearly like to have had someone to help me improve my riding during my formative years.

Not having an ideal figure for riding, and not having been taught how to find the correct position in the saddle, I am probably more aware of the problems which arise from these deficiencies, and am therefore more sympathetic towards those who suffer from them. Elegant, talented riders seldom comprehend the difficulties which ordinary riders experience.

I hope that as an instructor I have helped some riders to develop a comfortable and effective seat, and I hope that this book will help others to become balanced, accomplished riders.

Pegotty Henriques

uthor's Note   I would like to acknowledge with thanks the advice given by lizabeth Adams, whom I consulted on various points connected with ıysiotherapy.

CHAPTER

1

Why does the correct position matter?

The way in which the rider sits in the saddle has evolved through the ages. Today the correct seat is based on balance and harmony: the modern rider endeavours to hinder his horse as little as possible, remembering that a balanced load is the easiest load to carry.

When the rider is balanced he will feel confident and will be without tension. His movements will become supple and fluent and he will be able to apply aids (leg, body, and rein signals) with independence and ease. Thus his influence on the horse will be effective but unobtrusive.

It is a pleasure to watch a rider and horse who seem as one. The horse looks joyful, his ears pricked yet listening to the rider, his back supple and swinging, his paces showing spring and life. He accepts the bit without tension. He recognises, understands, and obeys the aids because they are clear and precise. The rider himself looks comfortable and at ease, and you envy him his horse.

But watching a novice rider on a sensitive horse can show a very different picture.

Involuntary movements caused by the rider's lack of balance can make him bump in the saddle, his sudden weight causing the horse to stiffen his back and raise his head. Similar irregular movements of the rider's hands and legs will upset the horse, making him confused, anxious and unable to differentiate between true, intended aids and involuntary, unintentional ones. Eventually the horse becomes used to continuous irregular movement from the rider and becomes totally unresponsive (dead) to all normally applied aids. The rider will then have to resort to force: probably stick or spurs.

This is hardly a surprising state of affairs if you consider how the horse's mind works. He is a generous, simple creature. When he was first backed he became used to a troublesome burden remarkably quickly; some horses who are correctly handled show no resistance at all. It probably took him about a week to accept a rider on his back without surprise or resentment. In other words, he quickly accepted discomfort as a fact of life. It would therefore seem quite reasonable to expect him to get used to the constant irritations of a rider's legs and hands giving incessant signals. He will accept them as yet another fact of life in no time at all.

To improve our horses we must first improve ourselves, and the vital basis for good riding is a balanced, supple, established position in the saddle. It should be the ambition and prime concern of every rider.

Dedication and hard work are essential. The rider has a long path ahead, struggling to overcome physical difficulties and to develop the muscular control that is so important.

Because the horse is a living creature and makes frequent irregular movements, good balance is gradually achieved through feel, awareness and practice. Just as the small child slowly finds his balance when learning to walk, so the novice rider will find his when riding. It will probably take about as long, too, bearing in mind that a child spends most of his waking hours practising.

The way we expect our horses to go for us is so very closely linked to our own movements and attitudes. We expect our horses to be submissive: yet how 'submissive' are we about out attitudes to instruction and the training of our horses? Not only must our horses submit to our wishes, but to understand them we ourselves must be humble and receptive in our learning. Riding is not merely a question of mechanics. Once the fundamentals are achieved, it is more a study in sensitive understanding, of thinking through the mind of the horse rather than imposing our will on him. We must always be ready to know that somehow the fault is ours not his. When we ride we must submit our minds and our bodies fully to the horse.

We ask the horse to engage his hindquarters, and to achieve this we must engage ours (the seat).

We expect him to be supple and go with energy. But he will not be able to if we lack suppleness ourselves and are lazy.

We hope that his paces will be rhythmic, regular and free: but how can he be so if our movements are irregular and restrictive?

The rider will always be an influence on the horse which he is riding, for good or bad. Through feel and awareness he must learn how to use his body to influence his horse to his advantage. He must reach the point where he does not have to concentrate on or think about his position, and it is essential that he should do so before he attempts to train a horse. Once he starts thinking about how his horse is going, his mind will never again be fully concentrated on his own body for a sufficient length of time for him to make improvements of any other than a transient nature.

A rider must never, however, become complacent about his position in the saddle – for like paddock fencing it will need constant attention.

This is when lungeing can be of the greatest value, the rider being completely free to make corrections to himself.

Changes in the rider's body, such as growth or increased weight, naturally disturb his equilibrium. It is, sadly, very common for a young rider who has had a dazzling career before the onset of maturity to 'lose his talent' in a dramatic way.

He has not lost his talent: merely his balance.

2

The path to learning

It is difficult for the rider to improve his own position by himself. The use of mirrors or video cameras can be of great help, but there is no real substitute for the attention, interest and 'eye' of a competent instructor. To help a rider to achieve a good and effective position can be a most rewarding task.

The rider must also have a genuine desire to learn and improve, for tremendous mental effort is often required to overcome riding faults that have developed over the years.

I hope that in these pages you will find the encouragement and motivation to work towards achieving a better position in the saddle, and that some of the observations will relate to your own problems, which have been brought to your attention but not solved.

There is in the long run no real substitute for an instructor, especially one who has a quick appreciative eye and can say, 'Yes, that's good'.

The important link between the instructor and his pupil should be one of mutual satisfaction. The instructor must, of course, have good basic knowledge, and be confident in his own mind about what he is teaching. The rider must be anxious to improve, and humble enough to accept criticism. He must trust and believe in his instructor and must work constantly to improve himself between lessons.

When choosing an instructor to help you with your position, be aware that it may not necessarily be the person who helps you most successfully with the training of your horse. Obviously there must be a degree of compatibility between the two, and it may well be that instructors from the same establishment who have trained in the same system will be the most successful answer.

What is considered the correct position in the saddle is a less controversial topic than which system of aids should be applied. Nevertheless there are variations, so confusion – especially in the early stages of learning – should be avoided if possible.

One of the instructor's principal roles is to confirm quickly that what is happening at a precise moment is either correct or incorrect, and to convey this to the pupil, who can immediately associate the 'feel' of what he is doing with the knowledge that it is right or wrong. Through this the rider's own observation of what he is feeling is emphasised and forms the basis for the development of a naturally correct way of riding.

You will observe many different attitudes among instructors, so find the one who seems most in harmony with the way in which you like to be taught.

The good instructor will vary his approach to his pupils, demonstrating his understanding of humanity as well as of horses. I am frequently amused by the instructors who show infinite concern for the personality and temperament of horses yet treat every human being in a thoroughly callous way, with no consideration for their individuality. They seem to take the viewpoint that 'if it hurts, it's good for you'.

It is enormously important to choose an instructor whom you feel can also become a friend; there has to be the right balance of all the things you personally need from him. People vary greatly in their requirements. Some love to be bullied and feel that praise is a waste of time. Others, given the same treatment, would only feel discouraged and demoralised, and would go away crushed.

An appreciation of the physical limitations and mental ability of the rider is most important. The approach to a highly intelligent, rather arthritic, elderly rider would have to be quite different from that to an equally intelligent young athletic person. Nothing would irritate the elder of the two more than being patronised, yet a sympathetic understanding of what might possibly be accomplished or at any rate 'worked round' would be fully appreciated. The same rules might apply to the less intelligent yet naturally talented rider who does things instinctively. Here the body is no problem, but the knowledge might take longer to assimilate, so the input into the brain would have to be slower.

From an instructional point of view, the ratio of body learning to brain learning must always be considered. It is only when the two travel side by side that the body begins to act correctly through reflexes. Normally, in riding, most of our natural reflexes have to be overcome, and it is only after a period of concentration (brain learning) and denying ourselves these natural reflexes that we can overcome them.

Children learn to walk using brain and body learning, but principally body learning. It takes time for them to find their balance and co-ordination, but because their brain keeps on rejecting the idea of falling over, their body goes on trying to keep upright. In this case the body is quite sure what it wants to achieve. With the rider, the body is not always clear about what it should be doing. Here the instructor must play a helpful role and direct the brain. Simultaneously the body must be given enough time to learn how to function in a new way. Generally speaking, the body is good at evading discomfort, which may initially be necessary, so the brain has to overcome this evasion.

Having said that the body must put up with some discomfort, there are limits! Little will be achieved if the rider is either tired or aching. The good instructor will realise that breaks for the rider are as essential as periods of rest for the untrained horse.

Perhaps the rider should not believe that he must feel pain but instead should become aware of an 'unfamiliar' feeling that merely seems uncomfortable or unnatural. Sitting on a horse is not a natural thing to do, and – as with most other sports – new muscles have to be developed. Unfortunately the beginner frequently develops incorrect ones which have to be 'got rid of' at the same time as correct ones are being developed.

Some people are very tough, others tire easily. The difference must be appreciated, as must their degree of general physical fitness.

The rider may frequently become frustrated by his own inadequacies, and progress may appear to be nil. It is at times like this that the instructor is most under pressure, and must find ways to re-stimulate his pupil's enthusiasm.

Initially, when taking lessons, there is much to be learned and therefore enthusiasm is high. As the knowledge is absorbed and the body and muscular development sometimes fail to keep pace with the brain, interest is bound to wane. The good instructor will now find ways to encourage and re-enthuse his pupil. Despite the fact that progress is following the normal path, he may well lose his pupil if he does not.

The principal means of communication between pupil and teacher is through words. It is so very easy for an instructor to be quite sure in his own mind that what he has told the rider to do is absolutely clear. The rider, also, may well feel he understands perfectly what has been said – yet frequently a misunderstanding exists. It is therefore vital for two-way dialogue to take place, with the pupil re-explaining what he thinks he has been told. The question and answer technique can be very revealing.

New phrases and images should be used until the 'key' to that particular door in the rider's mind is found. As far as possible, jargon terms should not be used, for they add a great air of exclusion to those who do not know them.

For position lessons, it is essential for the instructor to understand the root cause of the rider's faults and not merely to become a vocal inventory of the rider's apparent inadequacies.

With discipline and understanding of your own problems it is possible to improve yourself. Constant instruction is not necessary – perhaps with the thinking rider it could even be counter-productive. Everyone needs a little time on their own to try things out for themselves, and the over-instructed rider may lose his independence and become too reliant on that voice from the floor.

CHAPTER

3

The rider's physique

Unfortunately some human bodies are more suitable for riding than others. Within the bracket of 'riding horses' different shapes are better for different branches of equestrianism.

If we look at two extremes – racing and dressage – and conjure up an image of typical examples of a rider from each, we will find a short, light, compact athlete on the racehorse, and a long-legged, slim, graceful rider on the dressage horse.

Very few of us have the perfect shape and there are a great many top riders in all branches of riding who have overcome problems relating to their conformation.

A long, slim leg which is proportionately not longer in the thigh is ideal, though excessive length restricts the choice of horses. The feet should be set on to the leg pointing directly forwards. The thigh itself will lie well on the saddle if it is slim and if the inside muscle is flat. Correct riding will develop this flatness anyway.

Slimness, in general, is attractive and an advantage, but over-narrow hips can hold the rider's legs so that they come from too narrow a base and make it difficult for them to sit on anything but a narrow horse. It is hard for them to 'get their legs round' the horse and they will have a tendency to pinch upwards with a tightened thigh.

The thigh bone ends in the hip joint, which is part of the pelvic girdle. This is a ball-and-socket type joint that allows a very wide range of movement of the leg. It can be moved forwards, sideways and backwards and is fully rotational. The limitations of movement relate to suppleness, and it is in this joint that, for the rider, a wide range of movement is a particular advantage.

Generally the body of the rider, particularly the upper body, should not be too long, especially from seat bones to the top of the hip, as this raises the centre of gravity and can produce an over-exaggerated back

*Anne-Grethe Jensen riding Marzog at Aachen in 1985. Jensen, who has
an ideal shape for dressage riding, has a superb position here. To be
over-critical one might say that there was more weight on the inside of her
foot than on the outside.*

movement. The compact upper body and long, slim leg is ideal, though
there are large numbers of riders who disprove this theory. Perfect
balance is much more difficult to achieve if there is top heaviness. Heavy
shoulders or – with women – large breasts, can produce the same sort of
over-balancing effect.

The rider's back has to be supple yet strong. The person who has good
self-carriage when walking or sitting will generally be equally upright
when sitting on a horse. By upright I do not imply the military attitude of
standing to attention with shoulders braced; the ideal posture can be

This leading rider, despite having an impeccable leg position, has brought his shoulders too far behind the vertical.

likened to a stack of children's building bricks. If they are stacked neatly, one on top of the other, they will not wobble or topple over. So it is with the spine. The vertebrae should be well stacked, one above the other, the muscles controlling the movement.

Arms should be of reasonable length, especially from the elbow to the shoulder.

Finally, the head should be set directly upright. Most of us are born like this, but a lot of us pay insufficient attention to staying like it.

The rider is an athlete. He will therefore achieve more if he has an athletic body. He must be fit, not only in the medical sense but also fit for riding.

Dominique d'Esmé does not have a perfect figure for dressage riding, but her continued success in international competitions is an inspiration to everyone.

His muscles must allow him to be supple, his body should have an elastic quality, and though big muscles are unnecessary, those he uses must be of good tone: i.e. 'elastic'. A very frail body will not stand up well to the wear and tear of riding. An over-solid body will lack flexibility.

I have described the ideal, and those who match up to it will probably not be reading this book. Someone with an ideal physique will find the correct position relatively easy to achieve, whereas lesser mortals always seem to be struggling against unequal odds.

Fatness is the enemy of athleticism and balance. If you are fat you can do something about it: though I am full of sympathy, as I enjoy food, too!

Nothing, however, can be done about your frame. If you are the wrong

Reiner Klimke and Ahlerich in collected trot. Klimke has an ideal shape for dressage and is an impeccable rider, though he often criticises himself for bending his head forward.

shape you are going to have to find workable solutions.

Possibly the most difficult shape is a long upper body combined with a short, fat leg, which causes top-heaviness. The fat thigh pushes the lower leg away from the horse's side; even if the leg is short and thin, the lower leg is kept away from the horse's sides because the rider's knee lies well above the widest point of the horse's belly.

Short arms are another disadvantage, but they present a much easier problem to live with, even if the appearance is unsatisfactory.

If your feet are set on at ten to two there is nothing much you can do about them – except take care when you go through narrow gateways!

The very long thigh can be a difficulty in rising trot if the rider fails to compensate for it by allowing his upper body to lean a little more forwards, thus keeping his centre of gravity over the balls of his feet.

Most novice riders have undeveloped riding muscles – i.e. the muscles which they use only when they ride. There are quite a lot of these muscles, which is why we feel stiff when we have not been riding for some time.

There are certain movements that the rider is required to make which, as far as I can discover, relate only to being on a horse.

The body has to learn how to do new things and, in some cases, to try to discard its more natural reactions. Everyone has a sense of self-preservation, which produces automatic, though sometimes incorrect, responses. The beginner always leans forward when he wants to stop. Even the sophisticated rider falls back on automatic pilot when he is in trouble. This is when the body has to do some re-learning, and it is only through constant reminding by the brain that the correct action will become instinctive.

Anyone lucky enough to have learned to ride on a well-trained horse will have discovered what an advantage it is, for the horse is always reminding them when they have done the wrong thing. Trying to train a horse at the same time as you are learning is very different – for you sometimes fail to get the right response even if you do make the right correction.

Only when the body has learned to dislike the feel of any incorrectness in itself can the rider stop concentrating on that particular fault.

So how do we set about this difficult task?

I believe that it is of primary importance for you initially to be prepared to concentrate solely on yourself. Do not attempt to correct more than one fundamental problem at a time, but pay continuous attention to that one problem. For example, instead of merely saying to yourself: 'I must relax between my shoulder blades', experiment occasionally by reverting to the way in which you used to do it, making yourself experience the uncomfortable sensation of tension, perhaps even purposely creating more.

I have often watched a pupil being corrected and instantly making the correction – as many times before. There is a fleeting moment of attention and, almost as quickly, the problem has returned.

Teaching your body the feel of what is correct is the only lasting solution. The new idea of the right feel has to be implanted into the subconscious. To get it there your body has to become more comfortable with the new feel than with the old.

Obviously with most faults this takes time, because the new muscles have to develop before the new position becomes more satisfactory than the old. However, when certain faults relating to balance are corrected the body quickly says, 'This is a much easier way of doing things. I prefer this!' and then refuses to go back to its old incorrect way.

Quite apart from a rider's basic conformation it is quite common to see faults which are related to injury, pain, physical defects, or unequal body development and growth.

Injury, even if there is no pain, can subconsciously inhibit the body from functioning correctly. This is the body remembering the previous discomfort.

Pain has to be dealt with away from the horse, as do physical defects such as curvature of the spine and crookedness with, for example, one shoulder being lower than another.

I have often found that very unequal and crooked riding stems from unequal muscular strength caused by development in a totally different athletic activity.

Two specific examples were a football player who kicked with his right leg and stood on his left, with the result that, when riding, his weight was always in the left stirrup; and a squash player whose muscles down the right-hand side of his spine were so strong that they lifted that side of his body out of the saddle first, causing an incorrect twist every time he posted.

It is a sad fact of life that some people are just born more unequal than others.

CHAPTER

4

The rider's senses

I do not believe that I am stating the obvious when I say that it is valuable for the rider to use all his senses: feel, sight, hearing, touch, and even smell – though not, one hopes, taste, as he bites the dust!

Perhaps the most complex of all these is sight. We need to be able to see in order to know where we are going and to assess distances, but seeing can get severely in the way of our other senses by being overpoweringly dominant. If our eyes are focussed too specifically our brain is inclined to be obsessed by what we are looking at. When riding this is a very frequent occurrence.

It is common to reject information which the body is receiving because the brain is over-involved with what the eyes are gazing at so intently – usually the horse's head and neck. Because the eyes are giving so much information to the brain it seems to be the only problem which has to be dealt with. The other senses are largely ignored unless they are clearly part of the observed problem. The rider who watches his horse's head move in a less than satisfactory way will also find it easy to feel an unequal rein contact. But he will probably fail to notice that his horse has stiffened his back. The eyes have much to answer for, and can certainly be blamed for the average rider's obsession with where his horse is carrying his head and neck and whether or not he is on the bit.

To experience the next most dominant sense – feel – it is often helpful actually to close your eyes for a moment. The relationship between sight and feel is very close, for we are inclined to expect and correctly recognise a sensation only if we see it first.

Try the following experiment on someone. Blindfold them, and then touch them with a dry ice cube. There is an equal chance that they will think it was something very hot such as a burning cigarette. And do you remember the children's party game of handing round familiar objects to those who were blindfolded? How hard it was to recognise what they

21

were, despite the fact that they were things normally touched every day.

Riding blindfold is unfortunately not to be recommended, but consciously not focussing is. Imagine that you are a wide-angle camera lens, and that instead of having narrow directed vision you are looking at as wide a landscape as possible. You can even let your vision blur a little. Now you will become aware of a more vivid sense of feel, that most vital of all ingredients when interpreting the way your horse is going.

There is so much to be felt. Quite apart from the information that your body is receiving about the way your horse is moving and responding, there is also the feeling your own body is giving you. How are you sitting? Where is your weight? Which joints are moving and which are still? Where is there tension? Where is there discomfort?

It becomes difficult to concentrate on the horse when so many thoughts about yourself get in the way and worry you. Only when your body is not intruding too much on your mind can you really feel the tremendous variety of information that the horse is giving you. Once you have assessed and processed all this, you start again to question your own responses to him. Was the aid too strong? Should the contact be lighter? Have you used too much leg, seat, or whatever? All these thoughts stem from 'feel' and frequently confuse the brain to a paralysing degree.

But, in reality, the aids are *touch*: how you touch the horse, how you make contact with him. What you do involuntarily is feel – and the first you know about it is when you perceive the sensation of your action – but when you pick up the rein you touch it; through it you touch the horse's mouth. Your legs touch the horse's sides. You consciously seek to feel him. This is where communication begins. He begins to feel what you are doing and the quality of your touch will decide the nature of his response.

Throughout all our riding we must seek to heighten our ability to feel what is happening underneath us and to our own bodies and, through doing so, increase the subtlety of our touch.

The sense of hearing is frequently ignored by many riders and instructors. This is a great pity for it can so greatly expand our comprehension and knowledge. Consider the paces alone and your assessment of how your horse is going. Certainly you can feel the beats of each pace, but the sound of them can sometimes reveal incorrectnesses that feel alone does not.

It is far easier to detect the sound of an unclear four-time walk than to feel it. This is certainly true for the novice rider, and listening to the beats will help him to learn the feel of them. If you ask a beginner to count the beats of the hind legs in walk he will usually match his voice to the front legs if he is on a soft surface. If he tries the same exercise on the road he

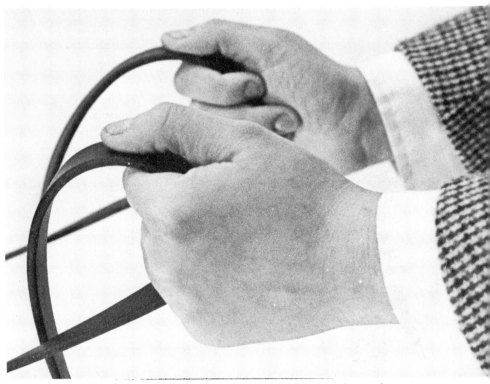

Hands in the correct position and experiencing the feel of the horse's mouth through the reins.

will become more aware of the hind legs and will learn through using the extra sense. It is sometimes hard to feel the moment when the horse departs from the three-time beat of canter to the four-time beat of the gallop, yet it can be clearly heard. The moment of suspension in canter or trot is another example of the advantage of listening.

Listening to the sounds of your horse's forelimbs in trot, and especially canter, will tell you whether he is balanced and light on his front feet, or whether he is on his forehand and almost shaking the ground as he puts his feet down. It can be of value to listen to other sounds that your horse makes – in particular his breathing, which can tell you much about his state of mind. The supple, swinging, loose horse generally has a rhythmic soft 'blow', gentle yet clear. It is a great reassurance to hear it, for you know then that the horse is content and working. Conversely, a tense horse does not breathe in a rhythmic way – you can sometimes barely hear him breathing at all.

Very often, after a short period of working in, when the horse begins to loosen up and to put a little effort into his work, you will hear him give a couple of real blows and reach down as he does so. After this, the regular blow often begins, and it is not until he becomes slightly anxious again that the sound is lost. Even something as simple as a change of rein can stop his total contentment.

The sheath noise from a gelding can be a sign of tension and, again, will disappear as he becomes relaxed, the soft blow from his nostrils replacing it. It is often quite difficult to know whether a horse is being naughty or is genuinely frightened, especially with a young animal. It is so easy to think that he is just being inattentive when in fact he is genuinely a little afraid. Punishment will only result in the confirmation of his fears. You can hear him thinking, 'I didn't like the look of that dustbin, and I was right, it's given me a pain on my side as well' (your whip).

Again, attention to his breathing will help you to know how to treat him. Snorting demonstrates genuine fear. You may even feel or hear his heart beating.

Grinding teeth is something that most of us would not fail to notice. If intermittent, it is a clear sign of anxiety. Some horses, however, have developed a rhythmic grinding. It is not really a demonstration of resistance, but it does perhaps tell us something about the horse's temperament, as does noisy champing, rather than soft chewing of the bit.

Though it may not be considered one of the five senses, I believe that the sense of balance must be included. Of course, it does relate to the ears, for our balancing mechanism is dependent on the interior part of the ear called the semi-circular canal. A good sense of balance is the single greatest gift that a rider can have, and the art of achieving perfect or near-perfect balance must be constantly pursued.

The human sense of smell is not greatly developed and we do not use it anywhere near as efficiently as do animals. Even so, it might draw your attention to anxious sweating. Sweat on the horse's neck only may mean that he is nervous rather than working hard. Sweat on his flank or shoulders signifies strenuous work.

Here I think we must also consider the horse's sense of smell, which is highly developed and can be a negative force in training. The horse could well become disobedient if he scented pigs or anything which he associated with an unpleasant or painful experience. He might be wary of the vet who had to give him an injection, and might recognise the same medicinal odours again. Your own awareness of these smells will help you to understand your horse's behaviour.

Not exactly a sense, but of great importance to the rider, is his own voice and the tone of it. Perhaps when using his voice he should also try to hear what his horse is hearing: better to keep quiet than to let your fear or anger be expressed by shouting. The voice can soothe, encourage, praise and reprimand but should never be used in an uncontrolled way. The rider's trainer can learn a great deal by listening to the pitch of and tension in his pupil's voice.

It is true that the horse does not actually say things to us, but if we are aware, we will find that he is telling us a great deal.

We must also learn to listen to what our own body is telling us about ourselves. We frequently push to the back of our minds, say, an aching shoulder, when in fact our attention should be fully focussed on what is causing that ache. Perhaps we are allowing our horse to lie on the rein; maybe our elbow is stiff. Whatever the cause, pushing the problem into the background will not resolve it. If you make yourself experience fully the discomfort, you are more likely to get to the root of the problem and therefore be in a position to eliminate it.

Your senses will help you to ride well and communicate with your horse to the best of your ability. You should make full use of them.

CHAPTER

5

The saddle: its importance and influence

The English hunting saddle has evolved into the general-purpose saddle from which two extremes, the jumping saddle and the dressage saddle, have been developed. It is important to understand the fundamental differences between these two saddles.

The single most important difference is the relationship between the bars from which the stirrups hang and the lowest (deepest) part of the seat. On the jumping saddle the distance between the lowest part of the seat and the bars is far wider than on the dressage saddle, allowing the rider a wider base of support. The forward-cut saddle flap leaves space for the rider's knee when he shortens his stirrups. With the higher knee position he tends to form a triangle between his knee, hip and head. In this position, to some extent, he loses the influence of his legs, but gains a wider and more secure foundation for his balance – like a pyramid.

On the dressage saddle the bars and the lowest part of the seat are closer together. The rider is therefore able to stretch his leg down, keeping his knee further back and more under his hip, and riding with his stirrup leathers long yet still at right angles to the ground. This affords him the maximum possible length of stirrup and the maximum influence of his leg. With the leg in this position, a forward-cut flap is superfluous. The rider's own balance is more difficult to maintain.

It is a common mistake to believe that a dressage saddle will 'put a rider into the correct position'. There are plenty of saddles that will indeed 'trap' a rider into the correct position, but this is far from desirable. Far too many modern saddles stop the rider from moving as much as he needs to, especially in canter, and therefore they tend to limit his ability to harmonise with the horse.

The ideal saddle is one that encourages and allows a rider to sit comfortably in the correct position, and offers a fundamental support on which he can balance himself. The worst kind of saddle is one that traps the rider in the incorrect position, forcing him to struggle against gravity in an attempt to achieve a desirable seat. Some modern saddles with high cantles and pommels, knee rolls and thigh rolls can act like straight-jackets. If the saddle fits the horse well, the rider – despite losing full mobility – will be held in an elegant position; but if it fits the horse badly, it will give pain to both horse and rider.

It is impossible to say that a particular make or brand is the ideal saddle. There is no such thing as a perfect saddle. Every horse and every rider has an individual shape, and each must be accommodated.

First decide upon the shape and size of saddle required by the rider. The size of his pelvis is probably of as much importance as the length of his thigh: the former principally governs the size of the saddle-seat, the latter the length of the flap. The very slim rider may well select a saddle with too small a seat without really considering the depth of his pelvic girdle: that is, the distance between the seat bones (*Ischial Tuberosities*) and the pubic bone (*Symphysis Pubis*). The depth has little relevance to whether he is fat or slim. A large or fat bottom will obviously require a more capacious saddle. The angle of the pubic bone in relation to the seat bones can also affect a rider's comfort and may make a high pommel seem very 'sharp'.

It is very difficult to choose a comfortable saddle without riding on it first. Selection in the saddler's alone is not advisable.

The length of flap is dependent on the length of the rider's thigh and lower leg. There is nothing more annoying than your boot-top catching under the flap of the saddle, yet a short-legged rider does not want half his lower leg on the saddle as opposed to against the horse's side. Again, the saddle must fit the rider's conformation.

Having decided on the seat size and the length of the flaps, it is obviously vital that the saddle should fit the horse to perfection. The number one consideration is the width of the saddle between the points, for nothing can be done if the tree (frame of the saddle) is too small or too large for the horse. Small adjustments can be made with stuffing, but anything more than a minor alteration will only result in a lack of 'balance' in the saddle and the rider being put in the wrong position.

If the saddle is too narrow, it will be high in front and the rider will end up sitting on the back of it with his legs stuck forward, feeling as though he is riding 'uphill'. If the saddle is overstuffed behind and low in front, the rider will tend to be tipped on to his crutch, and his lower leg will fall too far away. Only if, when the rider assumes the correct position at the halt, the stirrup leather is hanging at right angles to the ground can the saddle be considered correctly fitted and balanced.

Most riders are well aware that a too narrow saddle will pinch the horse and that an over-wide one will press on his withers, causing considerable pain and almost certainly giving him a sore back – perhaps even causing permanent injury. Less universally known, but almost as important, is the bearing surface of the saddle – that is, the whole area of the underside of the saddle which rests on the horse's back.

Though unfortunately seldom the case in practice, it is generally considered preferable for as large an area of bearing surface as possible under the seat to be in contact with the horse's back.

Some modern saddles have a rather small bearing surface, so that the rider's weight is carried on a relatively small area. Though it is not a good idea for the weight to be carried too near the loins, as with an oversize saddle, it is far better for the load to be comfortably spread. Think of the difference between sitting yourself on the top of a gate as opposed to a wide armchair, and of how the pressure affects you.

When the bearing surface is principally in the centre it is often noticeable that in trot the saddle rocks as the rider rises and sits. This is frequently due to bad stuffing.

Though considerable trouble and care is involved in finding the right saddle for both horse and rider, I cannot emphasise enough how important and vital it is to make the effort. Without the right saddle the rider is struggling against unequal odds, and the horse is in pain.

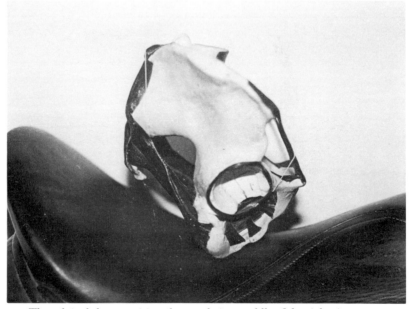

The pelvis skeleton positioned correctly in a saddle of the right size.

The central position of the pelvis. The position at halt and the positions which the rider moves through between figures one and three.

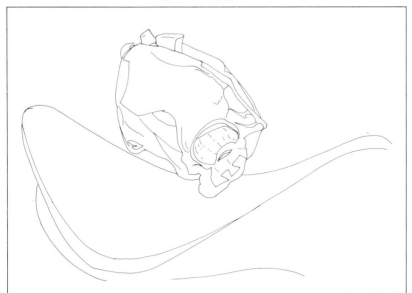

(1) As the back moves towards the convex the pelvis tilts further back and the cross-section of the vertebra is level (saddle correct size).

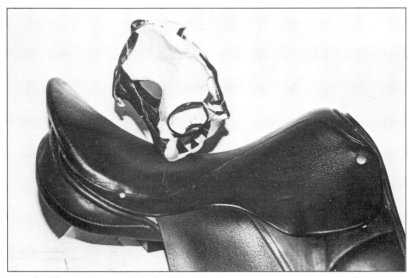

(2) The position at the halt. Note that the cross-section of the vertebra is near the horizontal (saddle too small).

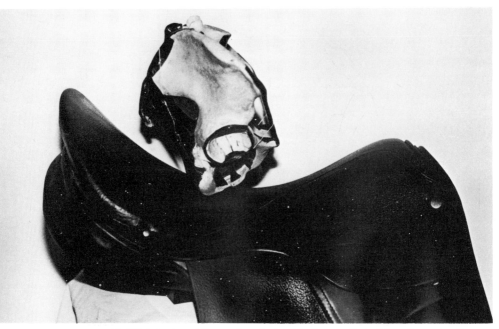

(3) Slightly tipped forward as the back hollows a little. Note the angle of the cross-section of the vertebra (saddle too small).

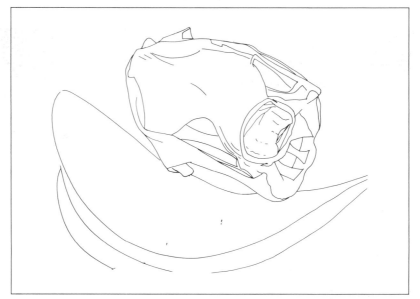

Sitting on the base of the spine. Note the angle of the cross-section of the vertebra. The rider's back would be very rounded and his waist would be collapsed.

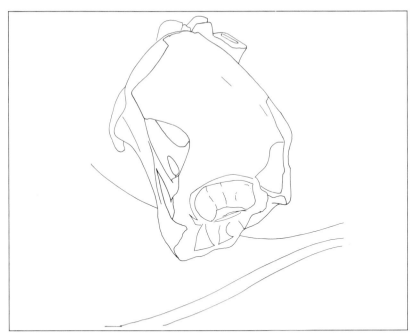

The pelvis tipped too far forward. Note the angle of the cross-section of the vertebra. The rider's back would be very hollow and the rider would be sitting on his fork.

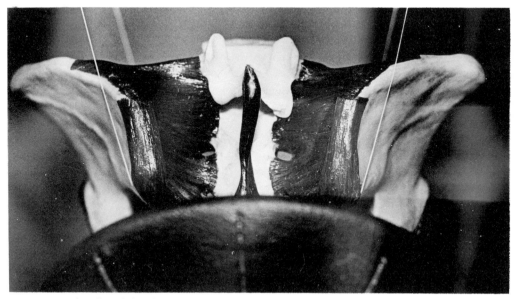

The pelvis from behind. This skeleton in a saddle shows just how uneven the human body is.

6

The correct position at the halt

There is very little disagreement about the classically correct position of the rider while the horse is stationary. It is only when the horse is required to move that the arguments and disagreements begin. So let us first consider how the rider should look and feel without the inconvenience of the movements of the horse.

The human being is at all times dependent on his balance to maintain any position other than a recumbent one. Sitting on a horse requires the rider to find the centre of his gravity and therefore his balance. The beginner's natural instinct is to cling like a monkey. The moment a rider clutches with his legs or hands his whole body becomes tense, especially his back and seat muscles. This rigidity foils his natural ability to balance himself. Consider standing on a bus that is moving and rocking about. If you hang on to something and allow your knees to stiffen you will not only have a very uncomfortable journey but you will also start to ache from the effort. If, instead, you let your body absorb the movement through your knees, hips and back – as though swaying in the wind – your passage will be far more comfortable and much less exhausting.

This is a good moment to differentiate between the hip joint and the hip bone. The bone (*ilium*) is where you place your hands if told to put them on your hips. The joint is at the top of your leg where the femur goes into the socket in the pelvic girdle. I will not complicate matters further by using technical terms but will merely say 'hip joint' or 'hip bone'.

When sitting in the saddle the rider must balance on his two seat bones. Though this is easily said, the smallest deviation to the front or back edge of those bones will cause loss of balance and failure to stay upright.

First, the rider should settle himself in the lowest and deepest part of the saddle, with his legs hanging limply down; then, raising his knees until his thighs are horizontal, he should attempt to sit absolutely upright, with

Left *The correct position at halt: a novice rider.*

Right *The correct position at halt: a more experienced rider.*

his shoulder and ear in a precise line, at right angles to the ground. He should not slump in the saddle nor strain to be too upright, but should conjure up the image of a puppet supported by a solitary string fastened to the centre of the top of his head. His back should feel like building blocks, with each vertebra balanced neatly on top of the next.

Now the rider should be able to feel the exact spot on each seat bone where it touches the saddle and forms his base balancing point. Having carefully memorised this exact feel, the rider should slowly lower his legs and slip his feet into the stirrups. He should by now be sitting without tension, with equal weight on both seat bones, with a controlled but relaxed upper body and a totally passive leg which is not being relied on to keep his upper body in position. The ear, shoulder, hip joint, hip bone and heel should still form the same vertical line that they did when his knees were high. If the top of the hip bone falls behind this line, the rider

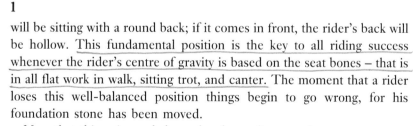

Finding the correct point of balance on the seat bones.
(1) The rider settles herself in the lowest and deepest part of the saddle, with her legs hanging limply down.

(2) The rider raises her knees.

(3) With the thighs horizontal, the rider attempts to sit absolutely upright.

1

will be sitting with a round back; if it comes in front, the rider's back will be hollow. This fundamental position is the key to all riding success whenever the rider's centre of gravity is based on the seat bones – that is in all flat work in walk, sitting trot, and canter. The moment that a rider loses this well-balanced position things begin to go wrong, for his foundation stone has been moved.

Now that this primary balance has been discovered we can go on to discuss how the rest of the body will be.

The shoulders and the hips should be parallel, and just for the moment the rider should let his arms hang down almost as if he had a bag in either hand: just enough weight to keep his shoulders down. This feeling of 'heavy arms' is important to the shoulder position, as any raising of the shoulders will create tension throughout the whole back, and tightness in the shoulder blades.

The rider's neck should grow upwards and carry his head proudly. The

2   3

head is one-seventh of the body's total weight and any way of carrying it other than in perfect balance will inevitably create tension and a distortion of balance.

The rider's upper leg (thigh) should now be lying loosely against the saddle. If the rider has fat thighs or if the horse is exceptionally wide, tension may already have begun to creep in. This is where the suppleness of the hip joint is important. Some people have very little sideways movement of their legs, so instead of their legs hanging loosely from the hip joint there is tightness. Until exercise has improved their suppleness, slightly shorter stirrups will help. If fat thighs are partly the problem, the manual 'pulling back' of the flesh from the inner part of the thigh to the back will also feel better. The thigh must be without tension, for a tight thigh means a tight knee, and then inevitably the lower leg is forced away from the horse's sides.

The lower leg should maintain a contact with the horse's sides that is

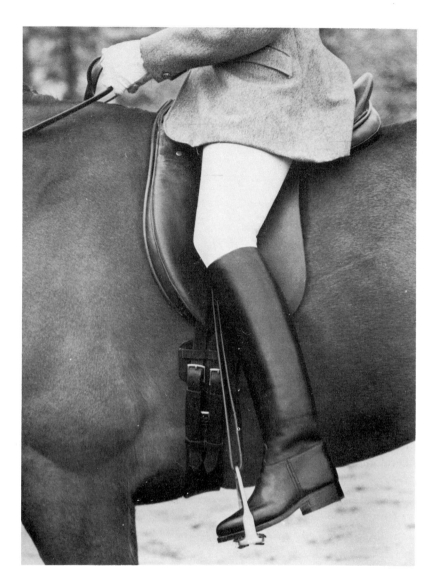

not restrictive. This contact should be able to 'breathe' with the horse and should not hold it in a vice.

The positioning of the whole of the leg is dependent on the conformation of both the horse and the rider. The deep-girthed or flat-sided horse and the short- or long-legged rider together produce such variances that it quickly becomes obvious that there is no such thing as the definitive position or length of stirrup. Though we may admire and seek to emulate the elegant rider on the well-shaped horse, we must be realistic and make adjustments for conformation defects. I believe that the constant lengthening of leathers which seems to be so sought after in the interests of a deep seat is often counter-productive. Far better, if in doubt, to ride a hole shorter and have good balance that allows the seat muscles to relax, than to ride with a hole too long and have an unbalanced, tenser seat.

The ball of the foot should rest with modest pressure on the stirrup, and the toes should point almost directly forwards. The weight should be equally distributed across the whole of the ball of the foot, and there should never be more pressure on the inside edge, for this will drive the leg away from the horse's sides. Particular care must be taken to see that the ankle is not bent inwards or outwards, as this stops the ankle being elastic and acting as a shock absorber. The ankle joint must retain its flexibility.

The weight must be equally distributed not only across the ball of the foot but also equally between the ball of the foot and into the heel. If the heel is not receiving weight through the ball of the foot, it will not be lower than the toes, then the rider's calf muscles will be slack and he will not be able to give precise aids. Only when the rider is balanced and his thigh and knee 'soft' can his lower leg express the delicacy of aids that are the horseman's ultimate aim. The legs are not weapons of force, they are the means of conveying subtle messages to the horse. Just as, with training, the rein aids become more sensitive so we should seek to achieve the same from our leg aids. If the rider lacks perfect balance and therefore makes involuntary movements with his hands and legs, he cannot expect the horse to be attentive to light, almost invisible, aids. The rider should always be aiming to lighten his aids, and the horse must learn to respond to this more sophisticated form of communication. 'Gentle precision' should be at the forefront of our minds.

I have left the arms and the hands until last because they are so frequently only a manifestation of what the rest of the rider's body is doing – or failing to do.

First, the position of the hands. From allowing his arm to hang down with 'heavy hands' the rider merely bends his elbows and moves his hands directly towards the horse's mouth, forming a direct line elbow-hand-horse's mouth. The rein passes directly from the bit, between the little finger and the ring finger, through the palm of the hand and over the index finger, the loop of rein between the two hands dropping down on the horse's neck. The rein should be held principally by the ring finger, the two edges being held against the hand and the finger. The four nails of each hand should look towards each other and the thumb should be on top, pointing towards the horse's mouth. Riders frequently ride with a delicate feel and 'open' fingers, believing that this is sympathetic. In fact, closed fingers are correct: they offer a more secure, sure contact that is generally welcomed by the horse.

The elbow should never come behind the vertical line formed by the rider's heel, hip and shoulder, and the elbow joint should move reciprocally with the shoulder joint, allowing the line elbow-hand-horse's mouth to be maintained at all times. The forearm forms a line with the back of the hand and there should be no stiffness in the wrist joint.

Seen from above, the line from the elbow down the forearm and hand should again be directly towards the horse's mouth and not broken by one hand crossing the withers or drawing sideways, or by the hands being held too far apart or too close together.

The fundamental riding position described above has not been 'dreamed up' to make life difficult. Quite the contrary. It has evolved over a long period of time as the most effective way of sitting and the best position from which the rider can influence the horse for their mutual comfort.

Experienced riders will deny that any effort whatsoever is required when this basic position is assumed. Their muscles have sufficient tone and elasticity to allow them to sit 'naturally' in this way. The beginner has to educate his body so that no strain is felt when new, previously unused muscles are put into use. It is the tone of the muscles that must improve; horsemen do not require large muscles, merely well-tuned ones.

However, it is not only a question of developing muscle tone. When bad riding has become a habit it may be necessary actually to lose some muscle. Just as with the horse who has developed a large muscle under his neck through carrying his head incorrectly, so the rider must let some of his muscles become inactive. As long as a strong set of muscles are fighting against the rider's desire to use a new, weak set of muscles, there is bound to be considerable discomfort and tension.

Any correctly controlled movement of the body is dependent on the co-ordinated use of muscles, in two ways: as 'prime movers' and as 'antagonistics'. Prime movers initiate the movement by contracting, while the antagonistics, also by contracting, control the degree of movement. Muscles also tend to protect, just as when we have an injury to, say, our back, the muscle in the surrounding area will go into a spasm. Our muscles frequently stop us from making a movement if they consider it night be risky, but sometimes we just have to tell them that we are going o take the risk!

Human beings vary greatly in their suppleness. Some people's tendons and ligaments allow them far greater range of movement than others. The very supple are lucky rather than talented. Undoubtedly everyone's range of movement can be increased through correct exercises – that is the muscles to which the tendons are attached will develop a greater ability to stretch. To some extent the rider can train his body to develop a greater range of movement through correct exercise, but limits will be reached.

Tendons principally join muscles to bone, and are devoid of elasticity. Ligaments join bone to bone, and in some joints they have a degree of elasticity. It is, however, quite possible to increase the range of movement by increasing muscle tone. Muscles only work by contraction. Because they have to contend with gravity, this frequently means that they give support. When you bend down to touch your toes, the movement is initiated by the muscles in the front of your body (*flexor muscles*) but the moment that gravity begins to pull your trunk forwards and downwards your back muscles contract and gradually stretch, supporting the weight of your trunk as you lean forward. They also raise the upper body by contracting more, and shortening. If, however, you lie on the floor and sit up slowly, it is the contraction of your stomach muscles that is used, for gravity is pulling in a different direction despite the fact that the movement in the hip joint is the same. When bending to touch your toes you will also feel the pull on your tendons and in the muscles down the back of your legs. This is the stretching of tissues which lack elasticity.

Despite the perpetual advice: 'relax', it must be understood that living muscle never becomes completely relaxed, except under the influence of narcotic drugs. Muscle is always under a slight degree of contraction. It is made up of a large number of bundles of fibres, and when a movement is initiated some of the fibres contract. The harder the muscle is asked to work, the more fibres it uses.

When it is in a very passive state only relatively few fibres are in use. Muscle fibre has the ability to shorten or lengthen by 30 to 40 degrees, and through exercise the rider can develop his personal maximum lengthening and shortening.

The rider cannot command individual muscle movements, for they are controlled by the central nervous system. He can only direct his brain to make a certain movement, for example, 'stop pressing your knees to the saddle'.

CHAPTER

7

The walk

Until the various gaits of the horse become familiar, the beginner will find the different movement of walk, trot, canter, gallop, and the jump, rather unnerving. It is a good idea to know exactly what is happening underneath you so that you can become mentally as well as physically in tune with the movements.

In walk, the horse takes separate steps with each leg one after the other. Because he has four legs and generally takes even steps with each, a regular four beats can be heard, and felt or observed, when the horse is walking.

His first step will be with a hind leg – let us say the LEFT hind leg. This will be followed, a split second before it comes to the ground, by the LEFT front leg. Then in exactly the same time sequence the RIGHT hind leg is picked up followed by the RIGHT front leg. The horse always has one foot off the ground. In walk there is no moment of suspension (when all four feet are off the ground at the same time).

The spine comprises a large number of connecting bones (vertebrae) which form a long flat S, ending in the skull. These bones have a varied degree of mobility, with the lower back and the neck having the greater forwards, backwards and sideways overall range.

All the movements the rider has to absorb when balanced on his seat bones will use the spine and hip joints. The movement of the rider's body in walk gives a good indication of the range of movement possible. The balance on the seat bones varies with each step that the horse takes, and the rider will find that he is moving equally backwards and forwards over his seat bones, his shoulders – in relation to the horse – remaining static because of the forward and backward reciprocal movement of the spine.

Imagine that the seat bones are like two golf balls which roll slightly forwards and backwards as the pelvis tips in rhythm with the walk. As the pelvis tips, so the stomach moves forward and back. If the spine remained static the rider would swing forwards and backwards from the hips, with the shoulders swinging like a pendulum. This would thoroughly disrupt the balance of both rider and horse. The rider would lose his balance to the point where he had to hang on with his hands or legs: possibly both.

Just as the rider's shoulders should remain still in relationship to the horse, so should his legs. The thighs and knees should be soft, and the lower legs, in pleasant contact with the horse's sides, should feel the movement of the rib cage with every breath that his horse takes.

In walk the horse swings his head backwards and forwards. This is a correct and natural movement, especially in the extended or free walk, when the movement is quite expansive. There is a good deal of movement in medium walk, but relatively little in collected walk. The elbows and shoulders allow the rider's hands to accompany this movement in perfect harmony.

Some riders can be a little over-relaxed in walk, allowing the horse to rock them from side to side in an exaggerated way, with first one hip collapsing then the other. This movement tends to go with a rather slumped position in the saddle, generally loose and lacking control.

Because the horse moves his legs first on one side then on the other there is a slight 'rocking' feel, as well as a 'thrust' as each hind leg steps forward. As the saddle is shifted both sideways and forwards at the walk, the rider tends to be moved in a variety of directions. To understand precisely how he should move, the rider must understand his own body structure.

The pelvis is the main mass of bone from which the legs and spine grow. From the front the shape is rather like a butterfly with the two wings spread out and the curves at the top forming the hips, while the tips at the base represent the two seat bones. Into the lower sides of these wings are slotted the legs. These do not, as might be imagined, form an upside down V, as the thigh bone (*femur*) has a right-angled extension at the top end which slots into the pelvis and forms the hip joint – the whole structure looking like an extended upside down U. From the side, the pelvis is quite deep and the spine runs into the rear part with a little 'tail' extending down (the *coccyx*). The front of the pelvis curves upwards and forwards (the *pubic bone*).

Another common mistake is 'pushing' and exaggerating the forwards and backwards swing of the pelvis into a thrusting motion, sometimes even accompanying it with more advancing of the hands than the natural movement of the horse's head indicates is necessary.

The rider's body should aim to accompany and harmonise with the horse's movements. Some riders inhibit the swing of the horse by being too still, others by being too loose. The aim is to be somewhere in between and to have enough control over your body to become an extension of the horse and the least possible hindrance to him.

Two actions are vital in walk: (1) The reciprocal movement of the hips and the spine, and (2) The interaction of the elbows and shoulders.

CHAPTER

8

The trot

When the horse trots he springs from one diagonal pair of legs to the other. The LEFT HIND LEG and the RIGHT FRONT LEG come to the ground together, then when he springs off that pair of legs there is a moment of suspension before he places the RIGHT HIND LEG and the LEFT FRONT LEG on the ground together. Again, there is a moment of suspension before the sequence re-commences. This movement is continuous, and should be rhythmic, with the moment of suspension dividing each lateral pair of legs. The beat is clearly two-time.

This 'spring' or moment of suspension creates a good deal of movement, though it varies considerably from one horse to another. Horses with lower action are easier to sit on, and they create less disturbance to the rider.

For the beginner, this movement seems violent and pitches him about, so it is better for him to start in rising rather than sitting trot.

THE RISING TROT

The rider raises his seat from the saddle as one pair of legs comes to the ground and returns to the saddle as the other pair comes to the ground. This is generally considered to be the easiest and most comfortable trot for both horse and rider, but I believe it is only comfortable if it is carried out correctly. It can be difficult for the rider and extremely uncomfortable for the horse if, because of lack of balance, the rider flops back into the saddle and, because of this semi-collapse, has to struggle to heave himself out again. The rider's weight dropping on to the horse's back will cause the horse to hollow and stiffen, and may be responsible for greater problems than a badly executed sitting trot, as the momentary weight is

43

The four phases of rising trot.
(1) In the saddle.

(2) Leaving the saddle.

far greater. (A hammer hitting a nail is more powerful than a hammer resting on the head of a nail.)

The major difference in the rider's position at rising trot is, of course, that his centre of gravity has changed. <u>Instead of balancing on his seat bones as in walk, he now changes his balance continuously from his seat bones to the balls of his feet, where they rest on the stirrups.</u>

It is helpful for the rider first to experience the rising position at the halt, since even this can pose problems for some. To begin with he should bend forwards from the hip joint without bending or collapsing his spine. Then as his upper body weight comes over his feet he should raise himself so that his seat leaves the saddle. His knee should not be straightened but should retain a soft angle. The angle between the thigh and the upper body should open but should not straighten completely, and the <u>rider should try to find the perfect angle at which to feel truly</u>

(3) Nearing the point of balance. *(4) The point of balance.*

balanced over the balls of his feet. He should imagine that he is standing on the ground and half getting up from a chair. If the weight is taken into the heels and not on the balls of the feet, the seat will tend to stick out and the upper body will be too far forwards. It will be discovered that the best balance is achieved when the hip joint is approximately over the balls of the feet. Until the rider can find this position at halt he will have little chance of achieving it at trot. Only when he can maintain his equilibrium whilst raising and lowering his seat can he expect his horse to be comfortable and the movement to be effortless for him.

When the rider discovers the point of balance, not only will he be able to lower his seat softly to the saddle but he will also find that the horse will be able to move him out of the saddle with only slight effort on his part.

Because every rider is a different shape, especially in the relationship between his length of thigh and his length of upper body, there can be no

Rising trot, seat stuck out. The rider is in balance achieved through leaning forward rather than bringing her hips forward.

classically correct angle for the rider to rise at in trot. The long-thighed rider will have to incline forward and advance his hip joint more than the short-legged, short-bodied rider. What is essential is for the rider to remain in balance throughout the movement and never to fall behind or in front of it. Judges and critics should concern themselves with this aspect of the rising trot rather than with the angle of the rider's upper body, which is only relevant to his personal balance.

If the rider persistently sits as the same pair of legs come to the ground, the horse will develop an unequal action, and those legs will wear more than the others. It is therefore obvious that the rider should spend an equal time sitting on both diagonal pairs of legs. As it is normal practice to work horses as much to the left as to the right when schooling them, it is a simple matter for the rider to change the pair of legs he sits on every time he changes direction in the school. It is not quite so simple when riding without clearly defined changes of direction – as, for example, when out hacking or hunting. Nevertheless, attention should be paid to this change of diagonals, or problems will result.

It is generally considered correct for the rider when circling or travelling to the *left* (riding on the left rein), to sit as the RIGHT FRONT LEG and the LEFT HIND LEG come to the ground. As he changes direction (changes the rein) he sits in the saddle for one extra beat of the trot and thereby changes the diagonal, sitting as the LEFT FRONT LEG and the RIGHT HIND LEG come to the ground. If this principle is used, the rider will always be sitting as the inside hind leg comes to the ground, but, as with so many equestrian matters, there is some argument as to whether it is correct. Some people prefer to sit as the outside hind leg comes to the ground.

Both arguments make sense. If the rider sits as the inside hind leg comes to the ground, his seat encourages the inside hind leg to engage more underneath the horse and therefore helps the horse to balance himself and make better circles and turns. Conversely, the inside hind leg might well be able to work better if the additional strain of the rider's weight were not added to its weight-bearing job.

I believe there is value in both arguments. The rider and trainer should consider the age of the horse, his state of training, and the relative strength of his hind legs. If a horse is particularly weak on one hind leg, it might be sensible not to sit at all as that hind leg comes to the ground, allowing it to develop strength without the strain of additional weight. Everything must be taken into consideration: the horse is not a machine, but an individual, and should be treated as one.

The rider must use his brain and work things out for himself. There are no rules that cannot be broken.

THE SITTING TROT

Sitting trot is the term used to describe the position of the rider when he rests on his seat bones for each beat of the trot. The novice rider should start familiarising himself with this as soon as he has achieved a reasonable degree of balance in rising trot – as long as his horse is not too young. Young horses cannot be expected to have strong enough back muscles to carry a bumping load, and they must be introduced to sitting trot by an experienced rider who has mastered the art of sitting softly and lightly.

The basic position of the rider in sitting trot is the same as his position at halt. The movement of the trot is absorbed by the rider's body in a rather similar way to the movement in walk, except that it is far quicker. Balanced on his seat bones, making sure that he is upright and not

Sitting trot: the correct movement of the back.
(1) Forwards.
(2) Upright.
(3) Backwards.

1

slumped at the waist with his head dangling forward, the rider allows his hip and spine to move in a reciprocating way to allow him to absorb the up-and-down movement of the horse. In a sense, this movement is initiated by the pelvis tilting forwards and backwards and the ripple running through the spine.

At present we are concerned with the rider's passive ability to sit on the horse's back in trot, interfering with him as little as possible. The use of the back as an aid will be discussed under that particular heading.

Initially, the movement can cause great discomfort to the rider and he will find balance difficult. It may be easier to re-construct at halt the movement which his hips and spine should make at trot. The aim should be to keep the shoulders above the hips and the head well balanced above the shoulders so that the ear is in line with the shoulder and hip. The seat bones should remain in contact with the saddle and the movement should be taken up by the hip and the spine.

The feel on the seat bones is important, for it is easy to develop an incorrect sliding movement backwards and forwards, the seat bones seeming to be on runners, and the seat moving backwards and forwards in

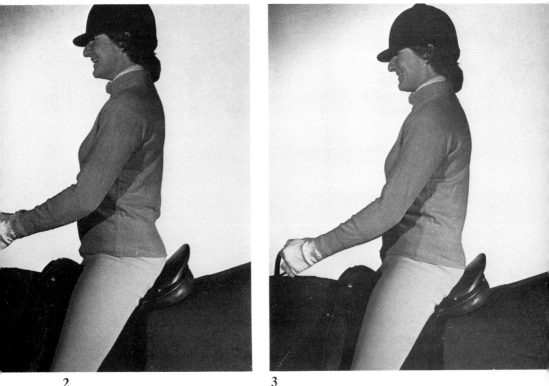

2   3

the saddle with an almost continuous pushing movement to and fro that is often accompanied by a stiff back. At its worst this also involves the rider coming well behind the movement and leaning back.

Imagine, instead, that the seat bones are shaped like two golf balls. As the pelvis tips forward and back the rider will feel himself rocking on his 'two golf balls' rather than sliding forward and back as if his bones were on two tracks.

The exact movement of the hip joint and back can be clearly felt at halt by hollowing the back, with the stomach moving forwards as the pelvis tips and the angle of the hip joint closes. Accompanying the swing of the trot, the back then returns softly and the spine becomes more convex as the hip joint angle opens and the pelvis swings back. It is important for there to be this forward movement of the back rather than the more commonly seen rounding of the back with the collapsing waist. If this movement is adopted the rider will remain balanced on his seat bones, and because he is balanced he will not need to grip with his legs.

Irregular hand movements and over-mobile or gripping legs are the result of a lack of balance. The rider will find great benefit from keeping his head up and not allowing it to hang forward. Because the head is heavy, hanging it forwards is particularly destructive to the sitting trot, in which an upright body is so important.

It cannot be over-emphasised that this fundamental position and movement should be thoroughly mastered.

CHAPTER

9

The canter

Compared with the walk and the trot the canter is an unequal movement, as the horse can vary the sequence in which he places his legs on the ground. When the sequence is the RIGHT HIND LEG followed by the LEFT HIND and RIGHT FRONT LEG together and then finally the LEFT FORELEG, it is termed the *left* canter and the horse is said to be cantering with the *left* leg leading.

When the sequence is the LEFT HIND LEG followed by the RIGHT HIND and LEFT FRONT LEG together and then finally the RIGHT FORELEG it is termed the *right* canter and the horse is said to be cantering with the *right* leg leading.

Generally, when the horse is travelling to the right he should canter with the right leg leading, and to the left with the left leg leading. This is how he would normally behave without a rider on his back, balancing himself easily and cantering about his field. At liberty, the horse usually changes the sequence of his legs whenever he changes direction. When this change of sequence takes place without returning to trot it is called a flying change of legs.

During the training of the horse, while he is initially readjusting his balance with the weight of a rider on his back, his ability to handle himself with similar fluency is diminished. He may well find it easier to canter with one leg leading than the other, or he may lose the described sequences of legs and become disunited. A disunited canter is extremely uncomfortable for the rider, as it feels thoroughly ungainly. One example of how his legs might come to the ground would be: left hind, right hind and right fore, then left fore.

Counter-canter is when the horse canters to, say, the right but with the left leg leading. On an untrained horse, this can also feel very uncomfortable for the rider, the horse probably being thoroughly unbalanced. After further training, counter-canter is used as an exercise to improve the horse's suppleness and to test his obedience. When the horse does the exercise well it ceases to be uncomfortable for the rider.

The novice rider must learn to recognise by feel when his horse is leading with the incorrect leg or when he is cantering disunited. He will only learn this through experience and careful observation. He must learn the 'feel' of what is correct and not depend on his sight. To begin with, co-ordinating the two senses will be necessary.

Having studied the order in which the horse's legs come to the ground, it is also important to understand how they *leave* the ground. The canter is a rocking motion, with the first hind leg coming off the ground as the last foreleg touches the ground. As the weight is fully borne on that leading leg, the diagonal pair of hind and forelegs leaves the ground together. Finally, the leading foreleg leaves the ground and the horse is completely, though briefly, airborne. During this moment of suspension the legs are repositioned, and as the first hind leg is preparing to come to the ground the withers become higher than the croup and the horse seems to rock backwards, so completing the full sequence of rocking to and fro.

The canter should have a clearly marked three beats as the hooves come to the ground, followed by a short, silent beat when the horse is in suspension. Though the canter is considered to be a three-beat pace, this is not exactly true if the moment of silence is taken into consideration.

Once the rider has found the trick of sitting to the canter he will generally find it very comfortable. In the beginning it can be jarring and unbalancing. The rocking to and fro motion raises first the horse's quarters and then his withers. To harmonise with this the rider must let his body remain upright by opening the angle of his hip joint as the quarters come up (it will feel like leaning backwards), then closing the angle of his hips as the quarters become lower than the withers (this will feel like leaning forwards).

With a reasonably well-balanced horse the rider's body should move equally backwards and forwards. He should in reality be keeping his body virtually at right angles to the ground, with the horse rocking underneath him. As he feels his body swinging backwards there will also be a forward movement of the stomach as the spine curves and absorbs the movement. As he feels his body move forward, so again will there be a reciprocating movement in the spine, softly backwards. The back and hip movement has to be fluent and reciprocal.

A common mistake in canter is to bend forward from the waist instead of from the hip joints. To counteract this the rider should re-create the feeling of having a piece of string attached to the centre of the top of his head, holding him upright without rigidity. Then he will lift his rib cage and swing only forwards and backwards from the hip joint, the back becoming concave rather than convex.

Any stiffening in the hip as the shoulders move back will result in the rider's seat being pitched upwards by the raising of the horse's quarters. This is the moment when a supple hip and back allow the rider to stay pleasantly close to the saddle.

Because of the rocking motion of the canter, there is, as in walk, considerable movement of the horse's head. It moves away from the rider as the horse's quarters come up and towards the rider as the withers come up.

The rider finds himself in the difficult position of leaning back and reaching his hands forwards, then leaning forwards and bringing his arms back. With a long-striding horse in working canter the movement of the shoulders and elbows can be quite considerable. With collected canter there is far less movement, as the horse's steps are shorter and there is little horizontal swing. This is one of the reasons why riding a trained horse can be so helpful.

Very often the rider feels – because the movement is so expansive – that he is giving the horse sufficient freedom of the head and neck. If he glances down, however, he may well find that his hands are static in relation to the horse's withers, and therefore that he is not allowing the horse any extra movement but merely acommodating his own body by moving his elbows back and forth.

Throughout the canter movement the rider's legs should, as always, lie quietly against the horse's sides, the knees and thighs resting softly and the lower legs breathing with the horse. From this position they are ready to apply any aid. Only if the hip is stiff or the thigh and knee gripping will the lower leg swing or bump about as the rider's upper body moves.

Balance is of even greater importance to the rider in canter, for he must move symmetrically on either side of the vertical, as does the pendulum of a clock, the swing of his upper body causing the sensation of rocking on his seat bones. He should in no way be dependent on his legs or hands for balance or support.

THE FORWARD SEAT

Once the rider is confident and secure in the saddle in canter he will need to expand his ability to balance himself by learning the forward seat.

It is used principally for cantering, galloping, and jumping, and it gives greater freedom to the horse by allowing him to use his back without feeling the rider's weight. Clearly, the rider's weight is still on his back but because it is taken mainly on the stirrups it is therefore further forward than when the rider is sitting directly in the saddle. It is also a more passive load to carry, for the rider becomes dependent on his leg aids and no longer uses his back to influence the horse.

To ride in this position the rider must shorten his stirrups, thereby bringing his thigh towards a more horizontal plane. This widens his base of support and makes it easier for him to be well balanced. Because the knee comes farther forward, a dressage saddle becomes impractical and uncomfortable for anyone except a very short-legged rider. A more forward-cut saddle will be needed to accommodate this altered position.

An easy way to find this new position is at the halt or walk. First, the rider should lean well forward and then slowly transfer the weight from his seat bones to the balls of his feet. As in rising trot, he will have to experiment and find his own perfect position where he can balance without any strain or effort. In this position the rider closes the angle of his hip considerably and, although he moves his hips forward, because his back is nearer to the horizontal than the upright, his hip joint is not as far forward as in rising trot. His seat bones should be close to but not on the saddle. His weight should drop through his hip, knee and ankle joints on to the balls of his feet and down into his heels. These joints must act as shock absorbers and must remain elastic and flexible and never be 'locked'.

When first learning this position the average rider will round his back and look down, which will help neither his balance nor his confidence. If he looks up and well ahead, not only will his back become slightly concave, he will also experience the same sort of sensation as when walking on a narrow bridge over rushing water and looking straight ahead to the opposite bank, as opposed to down into the water.

If his back is rounded instead of being slightly hollowed, not only will his balance be impaired but he will also lose the important mobility of his shoulder and elbow joints, as a rounded back causes a tightening across the spine and in the shoulder blades. It is vital for the hands to be completely independent of the body, and it is only the rider's perfect balance which will ensure this. The line elbow-hand-horse's mouth should be maintained, but because of his altered upper body position the rider will find that his hands are carried half-way down the horse's shoulder and much closer to the bit.

To maintain this position for several miles is very tiring for the rider, as a whole new set of muscles is brought into use. Pain may be felt, principally in the thighs and the lower back. To avoid strain it is therefore better to introduce this position gradually. A tired rider will flop back into the saddle, putting undue strain on the horse's back. This sight is often evident in the hunting field at the end of the day — just when the horse needs to be given the greatest assistance.

THE LIGHT OR MODIFIED SEAT

This position is a compromise between the forward seat and the dressage seat. It allows the rider to take his weight off the horse's back without his seat bones leaving the saddle. Though it may be difficult to achieve this position with very long leathers it is generally not necessary to make an alteration of more than a hole or two. Thus it can be managed perfectly well in a dressage saddle.

The rider leans slightly forward from his hip joints and takes more weight on to his thighs and knees as well as the balls of his feet. As with the forward seat, the hip joint, knee and ankle joints must remain elastic and the spine itself must not stiffen. This position is principally of value in the training of young horses, whose back muscles are not yet strong enough to carry the rider sitting deeply into the saddle. Some riders like to assume this position when approaching a fence, for it is very easy to resume the fully upright position if the influence of the back is needed.

CHAPTER

10

Fundamental problems

Specific rider position faults will be dealt with later, but there are many major fundamental difficulties which novice riders experience and share.

The most basic of all these is a lack of balance. This is principally due not to the rider's natural inability but to his lack of familiarity with the feeling of the way the horse is moving underneath him. Just as the sailor has to acquire 'sea legs', so the rider has to allow his body to develop an innate understanding of the movements of the horse. This is not something that the brain can teach the rider in a direct way. It is an expertise that is acquired through repetition until the feeling of all the movements of the horse are accepted as second nature. The body has to learn to make its own adjustments without the interference of the brain.

Young children learn to ride very quickly. Because of their smallness, their centre of gravity is easier for them to relate to and smaller movements are required for them to remain in balance. But I believe it is principally because they do not THINK what they should be doing and they are generally without fear or apprehension.

The human body learns to walk without recourse to calculated thinking of HOW to walk: it merely has to have the desire to WANT to walk.

But it is not so easy for the adult rider, even if he has followed the advice in previous chapters about establishing the feel of balance at the halt. The first movements the horse makes cause the beginner to tense instead of allowing his body to return to the normal point of balance, as a young tree does when it blows in the wind. This is not necessarily his brain getting in the way; it is just his natural survival instinct to hold on.

The best that the beginner can do to combat this tendency to clutch is consciously to make himself loosen his muscles and allow his body to regain its equilibrium. Unless he persistently does this, the muscles with which he clutches will become stronger and stronger and more and more

Behind the movement in rising trot.   *(2) Returning to the saddle (usually*
(1) Out of the saddle.   *falling heavily on to the horse's back).*

able to sustain continuous usage. The clutching tendency will then become normal to the rider, and his ability to learn to balance perfectly will be prevented. Only when the rider is confident enough on the horse to overcome his anxiety will his body be allowed fully to experience the 'feel' of the horse underneath him.

Joints and tendons are controlled by muscles and the much used word 'tense' implies that joints have become static through strong muscular contractions. As I explained in *Chapter 6*, muscles are never totally relaxed except under the influence of narcotics. Some of the muscle fibres are always in contraction. The real question is HOW MANY fibres are contracting? If more fibres contract than are needed, tension results.

But the rider who is relying on his muscles rather than his balance to keep him in the saddle will need to use his muscles strongly because they are fighting gravity. When you stand upright it is no strain. If you lean slightly forward without bending your knees or hips, gravity disturbs your balance and it becomes a strain on your back and down the backs of your legs. If you lean a long way forward, you will have to hold on to something to stop falling over.

This is exactly what happens to the rider. He is forced to hold on with either his hands or his legs. His knees and thighs will probably be tight, and his toes will turn out because he is clutching with the back of his calves. His hands may fix themselves on to the horse's neck or he may seek support from the reins.

These are extreme examples of a rider who has not found his balance at all. It is a tiring way of riding and is unfortunately practised unknowingly by a very large number of riders, to a greater or lesser degree. I strongly believe that the majority of rider faults stem from the fundamental lack of the discovery of true riding balance. I also believe that their problems are perpetuated by riding instructors who fail to understand that physical proportions and variable suppleness have to be taken into consideration, and who expect riders to conform to a precise pattern of movement.

Once the rider is fundamentally in balance he will realise just how much less effort is required to enjoy walk, trot and canter. He will, of course, frequently suffer slight loss of balance, and each time he does this his hands and legs are bound to move involuntarily as he regains his equilibrium. But as long as the rider is 'aware' of his momentary loss of balance his body will become more expert at keeping it. A rider's mind must always be aware of the feel he gets from himself and from his horse, and the inter-relationship of both.

The horse is naturally tremendously sensitive to the rider's loss of balance and to any movement of hands, legs, or change of the base of the rider's balance. Being the tolerant animals they are, horses quickly learn that these unnecessary movements from the rider must be endured.

Generally, when the horse first has a rider on his back it is assumed that he will quickly accustom himself to this strange burden. Few people perceive that the horse will just as quickly accept their bouncing hands, clutching or banging legs and constant change of balance. They are then disappointed when their horse fails to 'listen to' rein, leg and body aids, and frequently complain that their horse is 'not paying attention'.

Fortunately, unless actual damage has occurred to the horse's mouth or back, he will quickly become sensitive to small movements once he is ridden by a rider who only makes necessary movements for communication.

Again, I fear that some instructors are at fault when they constantly encourage their pupils to be more active and to work harder. So often it would be more valuable if the rider did less, kept his balance, and tried to communicate with his horse precisely and sensitively.

Certain riders when endeavouring to communicate with their horses resemble someone trying to have a conversation at a cocktail party where the noise level is high. You can shout your head off and still only a small percentage of what you say will be heard. Yet in a room that is silent you can hear yourself breathing.

Balance equals silence. Total lack of balance equals high volume noise.

A related problem, though one not due to lack of balance, is when the rider leans forward the moment he feels the horse moving. Again, this is quite a natural thing to do, and the rider is only following his natural instinct. The faster you run the more you lean in the direction in which you are going. The faster the horse goes the more the novice rider also tends to lean forward. He is not, however, out of balance; he has simply changed his base of balance, taking weight on to his thighs and knees. Unfortunately he has also lost mobility of his upper body for, due to the pull of gravity, his back and stomach muscles are brought into use to support the weight of the upper body, and they tend to prohibit supple spinal and hip joint movement. It is often quite difficult to convince such riders that, when persuaded into a visually upright position, they are not in fact leaning backwards. Leaning forwards has become so natural to them that a truly upright position seems false.

Tension is the enemy of good riding. Not only does it prohibit easy controlled movement of the rider's joints but it also blocks the rider's feel of how the horse is moving. Whilst good balance helps the rider to release himself from tension, it can exist in certain parts of the body even when the rider is apparently in perfect balance. This sort of tension or stiffness is often evident in the very experienced, trained rider. He and his instructor are aware of the problem but they continually fail to eliminate it. It is frequently due to a strong muscle compensating for the work that a weak muscle should be doing.

Take, for example, a weak-armed rider on a strong horse. He will not have powerful enough arm muscles to deal with the pull of the horse, so he will be forced to bring his back muscles into use to support his weakness. The shoulder blades will be pulled together and he will be forced to 'lock' or at any rate 'stiffen' his shoulders and elbow joints. The best that can be expected under such circumstances is that the arms will move stiffly; the worst is that his arms will become completely rigid. The fault is not the stiffness of the shoulders but the weakness of the arm muscles. Telling the rider to relax his shoulders will not solve the problem.

59

Before a rider has achieved a really well-balanced seat his legs may well flop about and his hands may bounce. His instructor, without first considering whether his pupil's balance is at fault, might persistently tell him to keep them still or at any rate in harmony with the horse. As a result, the rider, attempting to comply with his instructor's wishes to the best of his ability, uses strength. In other words, he forces his hands or legs into a rigid position, which develops those muscles that are doing the holding still, until gradually they become used to the extra work and the rider is soon unaware that he is doing anything unnecessary. The hands or legs will not have become more still – quite the opposite – and unfortunately the rider will now have an unequal muscle development that may stay with him for a very long time. Even very experienced riders have this sort of fault, which relates back to their early riding.

The loose, floppy or over-supple rider poses other problems. Usually his balance is good, but overall body muscle tone is lacking. Some parts of his body move too much and others, compensating, are too still and stiff. A typical example is the rider with the over-loose back and hip joints. This frequently exhibits itself with a wobbling head or clutching legs. The head wobbles because the upper part of the back is compensating for the loose, uncontrolled lower back and body by stiffening; this in turn causes the head to jerk. The legs are forced to grip to keep the rider in the saddle.

The beginner should first find his balance on the horse. Ideally he will do this on the lunge on a well-trained lunge horse. He will then be able to ride without reins and discover for himself his centre of gravity.

At the same time he will be well advised to develop better general body muscle tone by doing frequent suitable exercises *On The Ground.*

CHAPTER

11

Introduction to the application of the aids

I do not propose to discuss a specific system of aids in this chapter, but rather to discuss and propound various theories, and offer my own beliefs.

Over the centuries, through different cavalry schools, various systems have evolved, especially from Germany, France, Sweden, and the Spanish School in Vienna. There have been great riders who have developed and executed these systems or whose thoughts have been in tune with them.

There are still some cavalry schools in existence which have adhered to their great classical principles, but generally speaking the trend is for brilliant riders to develop slight variations on the classical themes, and these variations tend to get 'handed on'.

It is easy to see how the current confusion exists. Because of the modern system of 'visiting' instructors, riders seldom have the opportunity to go to one instructor on a regular basis. They tend to glean a bit of information here and a bit there instead of learning one classical system in a well-ordered way.

Current fashions in riding are inclined to follow current success and can be somewhat self-perpetuating, as successful nations also tend to dominate the judging scene. I do not imply that they mark their own riders higher: merely that they prefer their own because they are more accustomed to seeing them.

As I have mentioned in previous chapters, the horse is a highly sensitive creature. He also has a remarkably good memory. It is therefore possible to train a horse to *any* system of aids. There is no magic involved with any one system. It is the rider's ability to apply aids precisely, logically, and without confusing the horse with other extraneous movements of his own body which brings success.

It is obviously more aesthetically pleasing if aids are applied with subtlety: more pleasant, too, for the horse. It is also clear that the less a rider disturbs his horse by shifting his weight or with expansive aids, the less he hampers him with the burden of his weight.

Riders often think that they have discovered something that will revolutionise the way their horse will go when a new instructor tells them a different way of applying an aid and when they therefore get a strong response. The initial effect may well be good, and the horse may respond with vigour, but if the primary fault is the rider's insensitive use of aids, the horse will quickly become dull to the new one. I am referring to such 'aids' as the altered placement of a leg.

For better or worse the rider uses his entire body in his influence over the horse. Generally speaking, the aids are broken down into parts: the legs, the seat, the body, the hands and the voice. It is often stated that their independent use is vital: in other words, that a rider must be capable of making unrelated movements with separate parts of his anatomy. This is, of course, correct, yet I personally prefer to think of the aids as 'communicating' with each other, one supporting the other, rather than being totally independent. They must inter-relate, blend and harmonise. Separate use, particularly of the hands, spells disaster.

Unfortunately, the beginner tends to think first and foremost of his hands. He wants to know how to stop before he learns anything else. The horse, however, is not a motor-car. The bit inflicts a degree of discomfort or pain on the horse, proportional to how delicately or strongly it is used. His natural instinct is to run away from the pain, and young untrained horses will indeed do this. It is only when a horse is trained to understand the restraining effect of the rein aids that increasing the pull on them will have any effect. When he has reached this stage of training he should also have learned the far more important weight aids, given by the rider's body. These, together with the leg aids, are of greater influence and importance than the hands.

The voice plays a totally different yet completely supporting role. It is forbidden in all dressage competitions, even at the most novice levels. In training, however, used correctly it can serve the rider in many ways.

Its principal use is to praise or calm the horse; it can, however, be used to scold. The pitch and expression, rather than specific words, are what convey our feelings to our horses. Soft, melodious, caressing tones are calming and pleasing. A purposeful 'steady' can soon be understood as can 'halt'. A sound like B-r-r-r- is frequently used for downward transitions. A small 'growl' can signify displeasure. The simple commands given to the young horse on the lunge can be transferred, with advantage, to the rider's use from the saddle.

It is essential for the rider to use his voice as precisely as he uses any other aids. He should not 'chat' to his horse but should convey exactly what he feels or requires with unconfusing clarity. Some riders express their own feelings as if they were talking to another human being. This is quite incomprehensible to a horse. Just remember that a horse knows only the limited number of words which you use frequently and always in an expressive tone of voice.

I have heard a highly strung rider repeating 'good boy, good boy' in a cuckoo-like way that clearly conveyed a desire to go faster, rather than her intended meaning. Tone is all important. The nervous rider who expresses his own anxiety by shouting or screaming will only communicate tension and anxiety to his horse. By listening to your own voice you can tell a great deal about your own state of mind. A high pitch communicates tension. By speaking in a caressing way we can often calm ourselves.

The voice can be a great help or a great hindrance depending, like all other aids, on how we use it.

CHAPTER

12

The leg position

The lower legs lie on a very sensitive area of the horse's body. The lower down the belly they reach, the more sensitive an area they will touch.

Their principal use is to influence the hindquarters of the horse, either to propel him forwards, to move him sideways, to encourage greater activity, or in some cases to support him and prevent him from leaning inwards. The rider must learn to use his legs in many different ways. Initially the novice rider will have difficulty applying precise pressure inwards without turning his knee outwards and using the back of his calves, or flapping his legs by lifting them out and allowing them to drop against the horse's sides. This is not suprising because the muscles required for this direct inwards movement are hardly ever used. How often do you press your feet together or move your leg in the direction of your inside ankle bone? The only people I can think of who have to move their legs inwards actually to push against something are football players, who dribble the ball with the inside of their feet, and swimmers using the breast stroke, who close their legs against the pressure of the water.

The initial requirement, and one which is of prime importance, is that the legs should be still *in relation to the horse's body*. In other words, the lower legs must move with the horse's sides, retaining the same point of contact. This is achieved through the balance and suppleness of the rider and not by clenching the legs against the horse's sides. They should embrace the horse's sides with what I can only describe as a 'loving caress'. They should lie like a wet cloth and not be held in a vice-like manner.

It is often said that the weight of the rider's leg (the strength of pressure against the horse's sides) should never be less than the weight of the rein (the pressure which the rider accepts in his hand from the contact with the horse's mouth). Though this is based on the sound theory of 'legs not

64

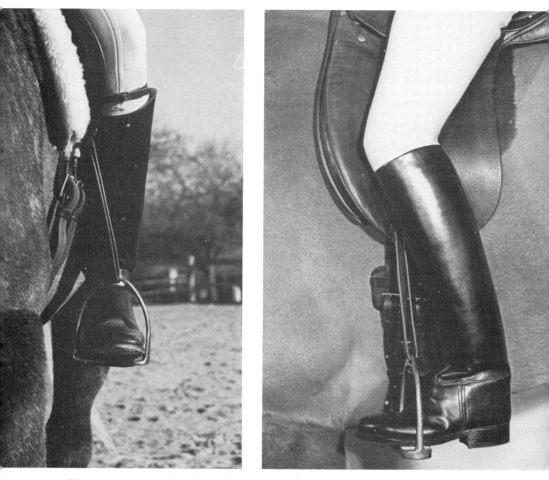

The correct position of the lower leg. The leg is lying softly against the horse's sides.

hands', I do not personally believe that the horse should be enveloped in a steel band to the extent that he feels restricted and unable to move and swing. If the rein contact is so strong that anything other than a 'gentle holding' of the legs is required, then the horse must be leaning severely on the bit, and corrective aids are called for. (Museler suggests that the contact of the lower leg should keep a thin piece of paper in position.)

This contact of the lower leg must not extend to the point where the rider bends his ankle inwards and holds his foot against the horse's belly. The rider should 'grow downwards' towards his heels, not inwards.

Establishing this contact of the lower leg is one of the very grey areas in modern teaching, where the conformation of the rider is seldom taken

65

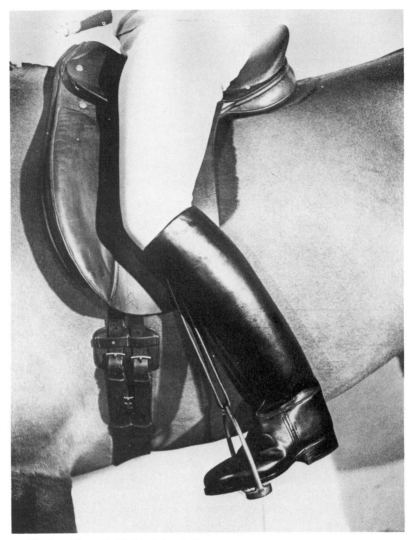

The leg aid applied behind the girth.

into consideration by the instructor. As I have already said, long-legged riders have an advantage because their knee comes on or below the widest point of the horse's belly, and so it is possible for them to bring their lower leg comfortably inwards in a natural way. The excessively long-legged rider on a small horse will have difficulties, for his inner lower leg will be underneath the horse. If he shortens his stirrups more than a few holes, too much weight will be put on to the feet and he will tend to slide towards the back of the saddle. He will have to use the part of his inner lower leg that is most convenient. It may well be closer to the knee than the heel. On a large or deep horse the short-legged rider whose knee comes above the widest part of the belly has only two alternatives. One is to ride with long leathers and let his knee open considerably, so that his lower leg finds a point of contact. The other is to shorten his stirrups a little.

From this contact of the lower legs the rider is able to apply the aids that his chosen system requires, without the horse being surprised by sudden movement. The leg may nudge, tap, press or hold. The ability to apply such a sensitive range of movements requires much practice from the rider, for this refinement of inwards movement is not natural to a human being. Unless the rider's heel is down, the calf will be flabby rather than taut, and too soft to apply effective aids.

These aids, applied inwards where the leg lies, are often incorrectly termed 'on the girth'. Of course the correctly positioned leg will lie behind the girth, with the rider's heel directly under his hip joint.

To generalise, all aids applied where the leg lies are either urging, impulsive, bending or supporting aids. When the leg is applied further back it is principally used to control or initiate sideways movement of the quarters, though some riders place both their legs back when asking for rein-back. This movement is made by bending the knee. Any tendency to grip or stiffen the knee joint will make the movement difficult. When moving the leg back it is important to keep the toe pointing forward, otherwise the back of the calf and the heel will become involved and the movement will lose its sensitivity. The horse should feel the leg moving back, but not experience undue pressure as it does so.

Some schools of thought believe that the leg should be moved back from the hip joint rather than the knee. I cannot believe that this is anything other than disturbing to the horse, as the movement must take the rider off his seat bone and thereby shift his balance.

Obvious leg aids are unattractive, especially the so-called 'windscreen wiper' aids, when the leg is applied far back behind the girth and reaches well up the horse's side. On the other hand, the leg aid position variations should not be so subtle that they confuse the horse. If the rider is able to be truly precise, his horse will understand him, whichever system of aids he chooses.

CHAPTER

13

The rein aids

There are many different ways of holding the reins, especially the double bridle. The way in which the rein passes into your hands is largely a matter of personal choice. What I am principally concerned with here is the function of the arm, wrist, and hand. For simplicity I will assume that the rider is using a single rein which passes into his hands in the normally approved fashion: that is, between the little finger and the fourth finger.

The manner in which the rein is held is important. The fist should not be clenched nor the fingers allowed to open. The rider should be conscious of the edges of the reins, not because he is grasping them but because he can feel them securely held in the area between the knuckles and the first joint.

It is a point seldom mentioned, but the rein width should fit the rider's

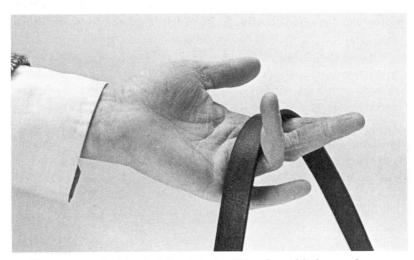

The rein must fit the rider's hand. It should be of a width that can be comfortably held in the lowest joints of the fingers.

hand just as his saddle must fit his seat. The width should approximate to the distance between the hand and the crease of the next joint when the finger is bent. Plain leather reins are frequently too thin, rubber ones are too thick; both will tend to slip. Some people believe that the thumb should stop the rein slipping through the hands by pressing down on the loop as it passes over the index finger. Others, myself included, believe that the ring finger controls the rein with the thumb merely acting as an extra. It is sometimes taught that the thumb should not even press on the rein at all but should be more to the side.

The rein is the communication link between the horse's mouth – via the bit – and the rider's hands. The quality of this communication is totally dependent on the rider's ability to maintain an unvarying feel on the reins whenever he is not actually conveying a message to the horse.

Human beings have developed the use of their hands to a very fine degree. Perhaps because of this we are inclined to rely on our hands far too much when riding.

The beginner should first concentrate on the passive quality of his reins, and in order to achieve this his fundamental balance must be good.

When he can be lunged without reins and feel confident that he can move his hands about exactly as he chooses, quite independently of his body, he will be ready to start communicating with the horse in a satisfactory way.

Any loss of balance will result in a varying rein contact, since human beings always re-balance themselves with their arms, even when moving on their feet. The horse uses his head. Riders use their hands. This is unfortunate, for often the rider's loss of balance results in the horse temporarily losing his, too, and if at that moment the rider's hands cease to be 'allowing', the horse will not be able to use his head and neck. The horse's loss of balance is therefore perpetuated until the rider has refound his own equilibrium. This can become a desperate 'chicken and egg' situation, especially with an anxious horse.

The rider who develops a true feel and sympathy with the horse's mouth is poised on the springboard of successful communication. Feel is the essence of a good rein contact. What the rider lets himself feel is what the horse is feeling. Sometimes we are so busy doing things with our hands that we stop really trying to feel. The rider must make himself aware of every variable movement which he makes and which the horse feels.

I often recommend riders to close their eyes at the walk, and to feel, without the distraction of sight, exactly what sensations the horse is receiving from them. If they can really follow the movement of the horse's

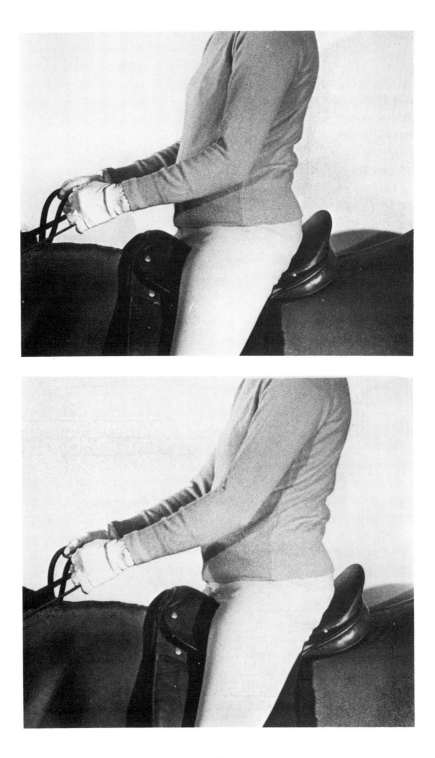

mouth with their hands without any 'bumps' they will be doing a good job. If they are aware of any interruptions to the purity of the feel of the contact, this will also be good, for they will be more than half way to understanding why the horse does not always respond to their rein aids. The average rider when encouraged to concentrate on just keeping a perfect contact will be horrified at how many mistaken signals he gives the horse through the reins.

It is not too difficult to write about this 'perfect contact' but achieving it is less easy!

Generally the rider is encouraged to 'allow', or 'let the horse take your hand forwards'. Little mention is made of the hand also coming back as well, so the rider is constantly pushing his hand towards the horse's mouth.

Though the concept of going forward is the ideal, in practical terms what goes up must come down. So what goes forward must come back.

This is the point at which I must mention the weight of the rein: i.e. the

Left and below *The movement of the hands following the movement of the horse's head.*

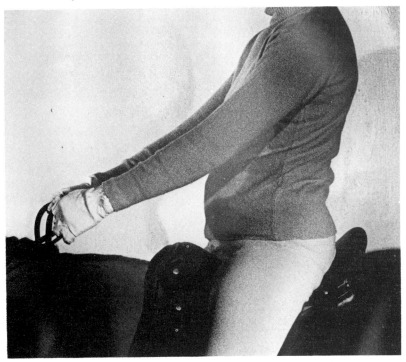

71

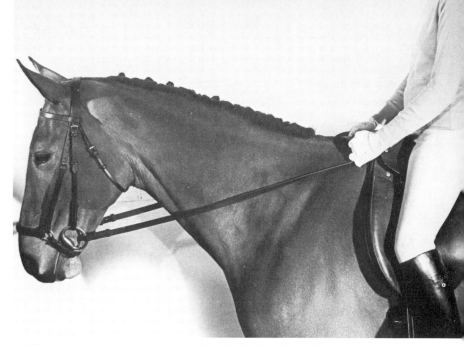

The hands touching the withers and held a little too low. The line elbow-hand-horse's mouth is broken.

weight of the actual rein plus the added weight of the backwards pressure which the rider puts on it.

I hate referring to 'backwards', but it is a fact. Imagine that the rider had the rein hanging downwards instead of out in front of him on a near horizontal plane. He would then feel the weight of the rein alone. Add a small object of, say, 2 ounces to the end, and the feel is then like the contact of the rein. The rider could move his hand up and down and the exact weight would stay the same. This is how the communication should be between the bit in the horse's mouth and the rein in the rider's hand.

All sorts of images can help the rider to achieve this tension in the rein without stiffening and producing contact variations. Imagine a plastic carrier bag in each hand with an apple in each bag. Hold the bag in each hand and discover that wherever you move your hands the weight (contact) will remain the same. Imagine a piece of string attached to the back of your elbow, which runs through a pulley way out behind you and finally has a small weight attached to it, so that wherever the horse takes your hand the small weight on the string has that gentle drawing back feel on your elbow. Of course it allows the hand to be taken forwards, but it also brings it back.

This means that there is never any 'slack' in the rein. Obviously the coming and going of a loop in the rein (slack) gives a horse a variable feel, akin to a rein aid.

Carrying the back of the hands uppermost causes tension in the forearms.

Having the reins too long produces tension in the shoulders and results in lack of control.

Once the novice has the feel of his hands being in harmony he will begin to experience 'feed back' from the horse. He may discover that the horse tends to drop the contact on one side and hang on to the other. He will learn on which side his horse is stiff.

Left *Arms still and straight. This is a common fault when a rider suffers from the illusion that she can position the horse's head with her hands.*

Right *Hands too high.*

No precise weight of rein can be said to be 'correct', but the rider should ensure that his hands are in no way supporting or restricting the horse's head.

It is helpful if the rider occasionally tests himself by briefly moving his hands forward so that the reins are given for one stride. This so-called 'stroking the neck' proves to the rider that he is not fixing the horse's head. The horse should not alter his carriage in any way with such a brief yielding. It is only after a few strides that the horse should start to stretch downwards and seek the bit. Conversely the rider should correct himself if his horse immediately takes advantage of the yielding hands.

Generally speaking, the more the horse is trained the lighter the rein will become, but the rider must be careful that the horse is accepting the contact of the bit and not, in fact, dropping it.

The hands receive and regulate the energy that the horse offers in response to the rider's leg and body aids. The way in which they regulate is by varying the otherwise unchanging contact, but they will have no effect unless the horse is ridden towards the bit with seat and legs. When the hands receive, and allow the energy of the horse to swing through his back, they will be in an effective position. Aids are then applied by squeezing the fingers, by giving small vibrations, by brief passive stillness,

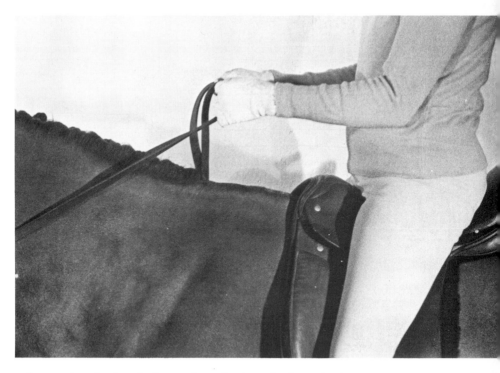

or by moving the hands forwards or backwards through the reciprocal movement of the shoulder and elbow joints. Lateral or horizontal variations in the basic position all make up the variety of movements which any system of aids may require.

As greater knowledge is achieved, the rider will learn to utilise the unequal effects of the rein and will realise why one rein should have more weight in it than the other for specific movements.

Wherever the horse puts his head, the hand should always remain in a line between the elbow and the horse's mouth. The arms should hang loosely to the elbows yet the weight of the rider's own hands must be supported by his upper arms. It is a common fault for riders to allow their arms to 'droop' as though their arms were too weak to support them.

The line elbow-hands-horse's mouth should also be visible from above: i.e. the 'bird's eye' view. Most systems advocate this, but there are some which like the hands to be nearer together. Personally I have found that doing this closes the rein against the horse's neck to some extent, so that the purity of the direct contact is lost. I have frequently found that riders who are having difficulty in establishing a harmonious rein contact will discover a better feel if they keep the reins clear of the horse's neck.

Some systems advocate the bending of the wrists, and in the past this was standard practice, all the subtleties of movement being entrusted to the wrist joints.

It must be understood that the muscle which controls the wrist also controls the fingers, and when the wrists are bent the muscle is practically fully occupied and the full finger movement is lost. Try bending your wrists and then feel how still your fingers are!

Once true balance, and therefore completely independent hands, are achieved a good contact will follow. After that, learning the enormous number of subtle rein aids is like learning to talk — and, as with talking, those who say the least are frequently listened to the most.

CHAPTER

14

The seat, back and weight aids

Before the rider can learn how to influence the horse by using his back and seat he must first learn how to sit passively in all paces. This has been described earlier under the *Correct Position* in the various paces.

Until the rider can sit harmoniously, imparting the minimum of influence on the horse in all the gaits, he should not attempt to use his seat to affect the way in which the horse is going. Otherwise he will never learn the refinement of the aid but will develop the habit of perpetually 'pushing' the horse along. Such riders are often described as having 'electric seats'. In other words, they are continuously driving their horses forward without realising it. Only when the rider has learned the art of sitting softly and harmonising with all the movements of the horse is he ready to begin to use his seat, back, and body weight to his advantage.

The use of the rider's weight as a driving, or impulsion-producing, force is controversial and complex.

Opinions vary about how great an influence the back should have. One school of thought believes that the back should not be used at all; another that the horse should be constantly driven by the so-called 'braced back'. Before an opinion can be formed as to what is right, it is necessary to understand the various ways in which it is suggested that the back should be used.

The movement of the horse is absorbed by the swing forward and back of the spine and the corresponding tilting forward and back of the pelvis, as has already been described at some length in the pages devoted to the sitting trot. It is very important that this movement should be clearly understood, for unless the movement is correctly made the use of the back will be wrong.

There seems to be a good deal of disagreement about how the strong influence of the seat can be applied whilst still retaining the feel of a flowing supple back movement. The common term 'bracing the back' can be misconstrued and it is perhaps here that the lack of agreement and understanding begins.

The degree to which the spine is mobile varies enormously from rider to rider. Many of the most elegant riders have wonderfully mobile backs; mobile yet controlled; their spines swing from concave to convex with fluent ease. These riders are most able to use their backs to create a little more momentary weight on the seat bones *without it being apparent*. They are able to add a little extra 'thrust' *when required*.

The controversy really begins over how and when the seat is used, and authoritative opinions vary greatly. Some believe that the rider's shoulders should be brought behind the vertical and the back brought into use by becoming concave. Podhajsky states: 'Wonders can be achieved if the body is inclined backwards when the legs are applied . . .'

Opposing this view is the theory that the back should be braced with a convex action of the spine. Museler, writing at great length on the subject and producing some very good images to give weight to his theories, partially supports the 'convex' theory by stating that 'the gravest mistake is a hollow back'.

Somewhere between these two theories is the thought that the back

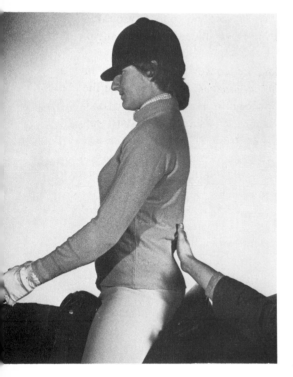

A hand encourages the supple back.

should move forwards and backwards with the swing of the horse, the rider applying the so-called 'bracing the back' aid with a concave action of the spine when required, the increased influence of the seat being at the moment when the spine swings forward — a sort of 'urging' with the stomach being pushed forward.

Out of this jungle of thought what should we believe?

Clearly the rider must first learn to sit without varying his weight in the saddle through bumping. The more he is able to harmonise with the horse's movements through moving his spine and hips, the more evenly spread his weight will be throughout each sequence of steps.

When he has learned how to do this, he is ready to start using his ability to vary his weight in the saddle to his advantage. The problem is how to increase the weight by a precise amount in a precise direction at the right moment without causing the horse any discomfort.

It is easy to see how in rising trot the rider can bring his weight down strongly on the horse's back; this frequently happens by mistake when the rider gets behind the movement and flops back into the saddle. It is equally easy to bump up and down in sitting trot with a thump thump on the horse's back, but this will only cause discomfort to both.

I believe that the stronger movement of the back takes place as the pelvis tilts slightly forwards then backwards and the spine moves from convex to concave. I also believe that the pelvis initiates the movement, with the spine permitting it.

When I use the expression 'rounding' or 'convex' and 'hollowing' or 'concave' I really mean a movement *in that direction*. It is simply that the back moves a little further towards hollowing or rounding than the normal upright position in which we should sit naturally. The back is seldom seen *visibly* to hollow or round. Nor is it really a bracing movement; that, to me, implies static. It should remain fluent, not harsh. The continuous movement to and fro is hardly interrupted by the increased push added at the moment that the spine changes from hollow to rounded.

There seem to be two separate ways in which the back can be used: 'the forward driving influence', which is obtained by using the back as described above, or the 'collecting influence' which is obtained by tightening the seat and lower back muscles whilst sitting upright. This latter action is the movement used in conjunction with the legs and reins to obtain the half halt.

The forward driving sensation can best be felt sitting on a chair with easy-running castors.

Your feet should be resting lightly on a part of the chair, but not on the ground. Drive yourself forward using a swinging, pushing back action which uses the back muscles, supported by the stomach muscles. You will soon discover that it is quite easy to propel yourself forward across the floor. This is the driving aid!

If you sit upright and use your seat and back muscles with a similar action you will only go up and down. This is the collecting aid.

If by mistake you use your back to thrust as it hollows you will find that your chair tends to move backwards. The back is often misused, turning it into the rigid driving aid which is so frequently seen in canter. Its over-use will only cause a horse to stiffen and hollow.

Like all well-applied aids the back will be most effective if it is used with tact and sensitivity and only when required.

There is absolutely no point in the rider even thinking about weight aids until his balance in all fundamental riding is good enough for him to be able to sit squarely in the saddle without sliding to one side or the other.

I believe that it is essential for children to learn to sit equally for a considerable period of time and to discover the 'weight aids' only when they are old enough to understand them intellectually.

The sophisticated rider will use his weight in some subtle, unequal way whenever he is not travelling on a straight line. The beginner should not attempt anything more advanced than a compensation for centrifugal force. In other words, to maintain his equilibrium.

Once the rider and his instructor are satisfied that a comfortable degree of balance has been obtained and can be maintained, the rider will obviously have reached the stage of riding when he is seriously considering the way in which his horse is going. By adding his weight influence to his other aids he is vastly widening his whole spectrum of communications.

The weight influence must be subtle or it will have an unbalancing effect, but its addition to the rider's repertoire does more than merely add another dimension. The whole spectrum of aids becomes more inter-related and the communication between horse and rider more finely tuned. The rider becomes doubly aware of the horse's ability to feel the slightest movement.

Once this stage is reached, the rider must start to react without thinking. His whole body must become trained to produce the correct reflex actions. It is rather like learning to drive a car. At first you think to yourself – foot off accelerator now, gently; foot on brake. But when you have become a good driver your reaction is completely automatic, even when you are in a dangerous situation. If you are a good driver your body will make the right decisions, apparently bypassing your brain. So it must be with the rider.

The greatest danger in using the weight aids is that the rider leans inwards when in fact he wants to put weight on his inside seat bone or inside stirrup. The result of leaning is, of course, that his weight slides instead to the outside, his seat actually moving across the saddle.

To put more weight on one seat bone the rider must feel his leg growing longer on that side, reaching down so that the hip and knee seem to go slightly downwards. His seat bones should not slide about on the saddle. He should be particularly careful to keep his upper body 'tall' on the inside, especially not dropping his inside shoulder and thereby compressing the distance between his armpit and hip bone.

I repeat again that in these pages I am not advocating a specific system

Turning to the right.
(1) The rider's left shoulder and hip are back and her right hand is pressing the rein on the horse's neck. Commonly seen when a rider is trying to hold a horse 'out'.
(2) The left shoulder and hip are too far in advance of the right. As a result the right leg goes too far back.

1   2

81

of aids. However, most systems seem to initiate a turn by putting the weight on to the inside seat bone, and generally all lateral movements have the weight predominantly on the inside of the movement. For example: shoulder-in right = weight on the right seat bone; half pass right = weight on the right seat bone.

Circles and turns are ridden and initiated by weighting the inside seat bone and stirrup. This weighting alone will produce a horse that is more inclined to bend round the rider's inside leg in a supple way. Conversely, if the rider slides, in error, to the outside, this can have the opposite effect by 'blocking' the horse's ability to bend.

Another grey and controversial area is where the rider's shoulders should be in relation to his hips. Most authoritative systems state that the rider's shoulders should be parallel to the horse's shoulders and his hips parallel to the horse's hips. This means that when the horse is on a circle the rider's outside shoulder will be carried slightly in advance of his outside hip. There are some who strongly refute this idea, believing that the rider's body should not twist.

I believe that this argument is largely academic, for the variation is a subtle one. I do know however that you will *never* see a photograph of a really top rider with his outside shoulder drawn back. This is a most serious fault, for it takes the rider's weight right off his inside seat bone. I therefore am personally in favour of the rider thinking about his chest facing to the direction in which he is travelling.

Just as the rider's outside shoulder must not trail behind, neither must his inside hip joint slide back, for this again will lighten the inside seat bone.

The influence of the rider's weight to the inside of the movement must – as with all aids – remain subtle and invisible. It is enough for the rider himself to feel a slight increase of weight on his inside stirrup and inside seat bone. If he can feel it, so can his horse. Stronger aids are seldom more effective: in fact, I believe that the horse becomes more and more willing and attentive as he almost 'strains' to hear what his rider is asking him.

CHAPTER

15

Exercises for the rider

As the average rider only spends, at the most, an hour a day riding, it is not particularly logical that he should waste that precious time doing exercises. If you look at it from the horse's point of view it makes even less sense. Here is that uncomfortable burden throwing himself about quite unnecessarily, constantly changing his centre of gravity and generally making life rather unpleasant for the horse.

But exercises are vital both to the novice and to the experienced rider, and are at their most valuable when carried out 'a little and often'. As I have said in earlier chapters, it is the *tone* of the muscle that must be increased rather than the *bulk*. Tone enhances elasticity while bulk equates with strength.

Every rider is physically a little different, and therefore exercises should be specific to his problems. There is a solid foundation of exercises which is universally helpful but, in general, riders will do far better to spend their time on those that are related to their own weaknesses.

Before deciding what has to be improved there are some basically important facts to be considered. Riders generally are stiff in one part or another of their body. They lack suppleness. This is generally an inability to move certain joints sufficiently or to stretch the related muscles. It is controlled mobility which must be increased.

Ligaments join bone to bone. Some have a slight degree of elasticity, and some, especially those in the spine, stretch more than others. The ligaments' basic job is to allow the joint to move fully while stopping it from moving beyond its normal parameters. Because we do not use certain joints fully in normal life their full range of movement can be lost. Correct exercise will help them to return to their natural mobility.

The hip joint is a most important riding joint and its full range of use must be maintained and if possible enhanced. It is the sideways movement of the leg especially that the average mature adult tends to lose through lack of use. The ballet dancer and the gymnast are perpetually increasing their range of movement and keeping their hip joints in full movement.

The range of movement is not purely related to the ligaments. Far from it, in fact, for attaching the bones to the muscles are the tendons, and it is most likely lack of muscle tone that produces the limiting factor and prohibits a maximum range of movement. The tendons are considered non-elastic, but they divide up and run 'fingers' into the muscles so that when there is a strain or pull on the tendons the muscle, if it is in good order, will either stretch and allow the movement, or conversely, defend the movement by holding.

When a muscle is in good order it will control and allow the movement of the joints through its control over the tendon. The rider must therefore concentrate his exercise on stretching rather than on strengthening activities. Most are more effectively carried out from the ground. Some are helpful on the lunge when the rider does not have to worry about the control of his horse; they usually fall into the category of movements which help the rider to find his centre of gravity and therefore his balance.

Very few are useful if carried out from the saddle when the rider has control of his own horse. However, there are some simple exercises which help riders to overcome specific temporary problems such as unnecessary tension.

Unfortunately many exercises inflicted on riders do nothing but cause further tension, loss of balance, and stiffening, and they are therefore far from remedial.

There is a strange masochistic tendency for athletes to believe that if something really hurts it must be good for them. This is really very untrue when it comes to riding. Forcing anything is seldom correct, and the poor horse generally suffers, as well.

The Yoga attitude of not forcing any movement beyond its normal range and of not working against the pull of gravity can well be applied to riding. Instead, making slow repeated movements until the scope and range of movement eventually increases, will pay in the end. On the following pages are some suggestions based on these principles.

For a short period exercises should be carried out several times a day. The body will then accept the movement and will develop accordingly. Just doing them for an hour once a week will have almost no effect. A word of warning, however. There is little point in doing exercises with a view to training your body to carry itself well on a horse if you spend the rest of the time slopping along in a slovenly way with rounded shoulders, sagging stomach, and drooping head. If you spend more time practising the incorrect than the correct, the incorrect will come out the winner!

The exercises should be carried out on both sides unless the rider shows particular strength on one side and weakness on another.

EXERCISES ON THE GROUND

BALANCING

There is no question that balance cannot be improved. A baby when it is very young has no co-ordination; its arms and legs wave about in a totally aimless fashion. Gradually, the nerve-channels to the brain develop 'routes', and the messages are able to flow directly back to the muscles via the motor nerves; the baby learns to walk, and gradually develops expertise in the control of its own body. Thus can the adult increase his expertise.

(1)   Stand with both feet together looking straight ahead, with arms raised and palms forward. Balancing on one leg, point the other toe, first forwards then to the side and finally backwards. Repeat with the other leg. Make the movement slowly. The object is to improve balance rather than range of movement.

(2)   Lay out a line of bricks. At first have them slightly staggered and a shorter than normal stride apart. Because they are staggered you will not have to put one foot directly in front of the other.

Step slowly – head up, palms facing forward, arms half raised – from one brick to the other. Try to step on to the ball of the foot, and keep your steps regular and even.

Once you can do this with the bricks in a staggered position, lay them in a direct line and bit by bit bring them closer together. The shorter the step you take, the harder it is to balance. Try to glance only slightly downwards, and do not bend your head forward.

(3)   Stand well away from a full length mirror yet near enough to be able to see your whole body. Look at yourself and correct any crookedness that you observe. Then close your eyes, shake yourself loose, and walk a few steps towards the mirror. Before opening your eyes, adjust your body so that it feels equal and straight, then open your eyes and check. This can be very revealing. Our brains can give us very false messages about straightness and equality. You may note one shoulder higher than the

other, or even find that you have not walked directly towards the mirror. You can make this exercise more difficult by holding your arms sideways or forwards and checking that they are equally poised when you open your eyes. Most of us tend to have one hand slightly above the other. Think of how this affects your riding.

SPINE MOBILITY

(1)   Though the following exercise involves the hip joints it is principally very useful in developing greater range of movement in the spine.

Kneel on the floor, supporting your shoulders on your hands with elbows straight. Keep your thighs and knees directly under your hip joints and your hands directly under your shoulders. First let your back hang in a hollow so that your stomach is relaxed and extending towards the ground. Then arch your back like a cat. Your stomach muscles will have to contract, but the muscles round the spine can remain fairly relaxed and a good range of movement should be aimed at. Do not force it. Move slowly. Feel the stretch, and enjoy the sensation. This exercise is good for everyone and is a pleasant way to start the day.

Note I do not recommend extending this exercise by lifting one leg out straight and raising it while the back is hollow, rounding the spine as the leg lowers, then drawing the knee up to the chin. This can impose too much strain on the back muscles as they must contract to lift the leg high. Your muscles will develop strength and bulk rather than elasticity.

(2)   Lie face down on the floor with your hands by your head, palms down, and a comfortable distance apart. Push your shoulders off the ground keeping your hip bones as close to the floor as possible. Now 'walk' your hands further underneath you so that your back arches and your shoulders lift further off the ground. Try to achieve a greater hollowing of the back without straining. 'Walk' yourself back down to the floor again and relax, before repeating.

$\rightarrow$ (3)   Find a convenient place from which you can hang by your hands so that your feet will be a few inches clear of the ground: e.g. a rail suspended from a beam in the stables, or the bannister rails on a staircase landing. Hang by your arms for a short time every day and you will find that those few moments letting gravity lengthen your spine can prove one of the most back-mobilising exercises possible.

(4) DO NOT ATTEMPT THE FOLLOWING EXERCISE ON A
SLIPPERY FLOOR.

Make sure that you either wear shoes with rubber roles or that your feet
are bare. Stand with your back to a blank wall or door that opens towards
you. Your feet must be apart and about 18 inches from the wall. Put your
hands above your head, palms facing forwards. Then, curving your spine
backwards place your palms against the wall with your fingers pointing
towards the floor. Let your head hang down backwards and 'walk' your
hands gently down the wall. In time it is quite easy actually to 'walk' as far
as the floor. Be satisfied at first with just a little backwards arch. Keep
your weight balanced over your feet by allowing your knees to bend. Do
not take too much weight on your hands, or you will become tense. Your
hands should simply be using the wall to help keep your balance, like a
bannister rail on a staircase.

HIP MOBILITY

(1) Stand by something solid, such as a chest of drawers, and rest one
hand lightly on it for support. Keep your upper body still, upright, and
well balanced. Making sure that you do not twist, swing your outer leg
forwards and backwards, loosely developing as much movement as
possible.

(2) Using the same support and a still, upper body position as in (1)
above, raise the outer leg directly sideways. The movement must be
sideways and not at all forwards. Do not worry if you have only little
sideways movement: it is far better to do the exercise correctly, as the
range of movement will gradually increase. Unfortunately, because of the
pull of gravity the abductor muscles – those which draw your leg away
from your body – will be forced to work rather hard. This is not the object
of the exercise; for it is just the increased movement which is desirable.

(3) Lie on the floor on your back. Keeping your legs flat on the ground,
widen them as far apart as possible then relax and repeat the stretch. Do
not overstrain. There is no point in drawing the legs together again:
merely stretch, then relax.

(4) Stand with your feet 12 inches apart. Keeping your heels on the
ground, squat. If you are supple, your shoulders can fall between your
knees and your arms can flop on the ground. Sit in this loose way until

you start to feel uncomfortable; raising yourself up and down only puts unnecessary strain on your back. If you feel no discomfort you do not need to do the exercise.

(5)   Sit on the floor with your legs in front of you forming a right-angled V. Put one leg in the normal cross-legged position with the foot on its outer edge. With your hand very gently press the knee down towards the floor, using a soft rhythmic movement which gently encourages the knee to ease downwards. Make sure that the straight leg does not bend.

(6)   With your knees slightly apart, kneel on the ground and put your hands just behind your hips. Lean slightly backwards whilst at the same time pushing your pelvis forwards and gently encouraging the movement a little with your hands.

LEGS AND FEET

Very few people have the natural ability to use the muscles which increase the inward pressure of the lower legs without cramping their thigh muscles. This ability is something the rider *must* develop. At first you are bound to become tense in your thighs and it will only be when you develop greater co-ordination through repeated use that you will appear not to use these thigh muscles (the adductors). You are, of course, still using them, but your control over them is refined to the point where the abductors (outward-moving muscles) balance the adductors (inward-moving muscles) and allow the knee to be fully controlled.

These are a few exercises that can be done without involving gravity to the point where tension makes the movement counter productive:

(1)   Sit on a hard chair. Let your knees hang apart and repeatedly press the inner edges (not soles) of your feet together. Keep consciously relaxing your knees.

(2)   Sit in the above position and pick up something such as a small, light block of wood between your feet. Move your feet about by bending your knees while you lift. This helps to eliminate the tension and to develop precision.

(3)   Sit in the above position but with the thighs well supported by the chair seat. Lift the feet clear of the ground and tap one against the other as rapidly as possible: the quicker the movement the better. As an added refinement keep one foot still and tap the other against it.

88

ANKLES

Some riders' ankles lack the ability to bend, so that their toes are held an inch or two lower than their heels.

(1)   Stand on the balls of your feet with both heels hanging over the edge of a step or a bottom stair. Hold on to something just to help you balance. Bounce softly up and down, letting the heels drop as low as they will go.

(2)   Sit on the floor with your legs in front of you and pull your toes towards you. Then relax, before repeating.

Note I am wary of advocating ankle-rolling, as I believe that it can encourage the ankle to bend inwards incorrectly.

FINGERS

Though most of us feel that we are quite good at using our hands, our tendency to be either right or left handed makes us give rather unequal rein aids. It is also strange that the finger most used in riding, the fourth finger, is unwilling to be used independently. Those who play the piano should have no difficulties.

(1)   Place both hands flat on a table-top, then raise the fingers so that the nail-tips are resting on the surface. Now raise the wrists so that only the fingers are touching the table and the backs of the hands are flat. Raise one finger at a time, and replace it. The fourth finger will offer the most resistance. Work both hands in harmony at first, as a pair from left to right: i.e. little finger (left hand), index finger (right hand) and so on.

SHOULDERS AND ARMS

Muscle tone and bulk is required in the shoulder areas because the shoulder joints are unstable (unattached). Riders who are physically weak or frail tend to stiffen their shoulders and elbows, and they even tense their backs, to provide sufficient support. It is common to see riders pressing their elbows into their sides and tightening their shoulders in a sort of muscular spasm. Stiff and straightened elbows can be another failing.

Only if the arm, shoulder, and related back muscles are strong enough can they provide the controlled fluent movement which enables the rider to offer the horse a good rein contact. It is therefore necessary to develop a modest degree of strength.

(1)   Use either two books or small hand weights. You can start with a pair of paperbacks and work up to encyclopedias.

Holding a book in each hand and working both arms together simultaneously, move the arms in any range of forward sideways movements, either with both elbows bent or with straight arms.

BREATHING EXERCISES

The lungs store and supply the body with oxygen which is carried by the blood to the muscles, enabling them to work efficiently. Failing to supply our bodies with sufficient oxygen can cause tiredness, weakness, and dizziness. Failing to breathe correctly can also cause tension. To use your lungs effectively you should use the whole of them and not − as so many people do − just the upper parts.

The lungs are enclosed by the rib cage and are large, reaching almost to the waist. They are attached to the ribs. To breathe well you must fill your lungs with air from the bottom upwards, controlling the inhaling with your ribs rather than by tightening your throat.

To breathe correctly:

☐   Stand upright and place your hands on your ribs. Exhale until you cannot squeeze another whisper of breath out, then slowly, expanding the lower part of your ribs, breathe in. Keep your shoulders down, letting your stomach, not your chest, do the work. Only finally should you feel the air coming into your chest. Now breathe out again, only this time control the flow of air by closing your ribs on your lungs. The operation of breathing should be through moving your ribs in and out rather than gasping short breaths into your upper chest.

When riding, it is important to develop correct rhythm in breathing. You must not hold your breath. Good breathing will ensure not only that your body gets plenty of oxygen but will help you to relax and maintain a correct body position. Breathing out lowers your centre of gravity and helps your seat to 'spread' in the saddle.

Next time you feel nervous, instead of taking a deep breath, as is usually advised, try instead to breathe out very slowly and steadily. It works wonders, and the breathing in will look after itself. We only hold our breath when we have full lungs, not empty ones!

CHAPTER

16

Lungeing the rider

Everyone knows that being lunged improves their riding position, yet very few people actively seek to be taught in this way except on rare occasions – when they feel pretty saintly about it. Why?

I have a strong suspicion that it is because when they have their first lesson or two it proves a painful experience. Rather like going to the dentist, they know it is good for them but somehow manage to put it off.

What makes these early experiences unpleasant rather than fun? I believe that it is because lessons are too long, too painful, and too tiring, and riders feel at the mercy of their instructors, pride stopping them saying, 'I've had enough'.

School lunge horses are frequently stiff and uncomfortable and the rider is seldom encouraged to provide his own saddle but instead is expected to ride in one that has 'been around for a while'.

The hard-working instructor may well feel he is giving his pupil good value for money by working through a range of exercises and paces for three-quarters of an hour.

But it is possible that the rider will get far more out of his time if a greater part of it is spent in discussing what he is feeling, how his body is working, and what specific problems seem to be troubling him. This should be a period of self discovery, of learning how to control his limbs and muscles, and above all of how to balance. All this should not be a strain. He should dismount at the end feeling that a key has been given to him to open another of those endless doors that reveal some new truth.

A good lunge horse should have reasonably comfortable paces, be of normal width, easy to control and obedient to the lunger's voice. The rider must feel safe.

The horse, however experienced, should be briefly lunged before being mounted. The prospective rider will then feel more confident.

As well as all the normal lungeing gear, a comfortable dressage saddle and a bridle with reins should be used. Side reins should be attached after the rider has mounted.

Only a very experienced instructor should lunge a rider. Not only is it difficult to maintain good control over a horse while speaking to and teaching the rider, but great perception and depth of knowledge is required to understand the fundamental difficulties and problems and their root causes.

Once the rider is in the saddle he should be allowed to get the feel of the horse in walk and trot, with the reins in his hands and his feet in the stirrups.

As soon as the instructor sees that his pupil is competent, the reins can be knotted: but they should be left over the horse's neck to encourage the rider's sense of security. It will give him confidence, too.

It can then be an advantage to continue with some rising trot work. This should always be carried out with stirrups: to attempt rising trot without them will only cause tension and stiffness.

Watching the rider in rising trot, with his hands either hanging down beside him or carried as if holding the reins, can reveal a good deal about his balance. It frequently becomes very obvious that the rider does *not* have an independent seat even at the rising trot. Time must then be spent helping him to find his changing line of gravity, as described in *Chapter 8*.

Plenty of work can be done at walk, to allow both horse and rider periods of rest. (Remember to give the horse a rest from the side reins, too.) I believe that it is especially useful to work in walk with and without stirrups, as this is the time when the rider can discover a great deal about the way in which his weight is distributed, exactly how to put a little more weight into one stirrup or seat bone, and how much weight there should be on the ball of the foot. He will discover a good deal about the way his back moves and the instructor will be able to check any 'overactive' tendencies.

Working without stirrups is of immense value, yet can be equally unproductive if incorrectly done. The emphasis again must be on the balance of the rider and the suppleness of his back in absorbing the movement of the horse. Any loss of balance will be reflected by gripping, crookedness, or tension.

In the initial stages of work without stirrups it is far better to keep the trot rather lazy, increasing the activity only gradually, as the rider discovers how to sit.

It is quite difficult for the instructor, on the centre of his lungeing circle, to see whether his pupil is straight, twisted, collapsed on one side, or unequally distributing his weight. One way to tell is by careful observation and comparison of leg and shoulder positions, first on one rein and then on the other. One toe turned out, one leg further forward than the other, a tilted head, or a shoulder hanging back are all danger signs which require more careful attention. Unless the instructor is very experienced he may find it necessary to get an assistant to lunge the rider while he observes from the outer edge of the circle.

Lungeing is generally thought to be the indispensable route to a 'deep seat'. I think that to some extent this is true because it encourages the pre-requisites of such a seat: balance, suppleness, harmony, co-ordination, and lack of superfluous tension. The opposing influence of lungeing is the rider's possible inability to find his centre of gravity and therefore his balance, resulting in the over-use of many muscles. This tenseness or stiffness develops into a battle between the muscles, which are known as the 'prime movers' (the contracting muscles) and the 'antagonistic' muscles (the ones which control the degree of movement the prime movers are making). Such a battle of muscles produces rigidity.

A deep seat is dependent on 'soft', relaxed seat muscles, relatively soft adductors (inner thigh muscles) and supple hips. This allows the rider's seat bones to come closer to the saddle and not to be pushed away or protected by his seat muscles.

The common exercise of holding the pommel with one hand and pulling oneself down into the saddle can result in tightened back muscles, and frequently in tightness in the seat.

Sit on a hard chair, upright but not tense. Now press your knees together very hard. You will feel your seat muscles tighten and you will rise an inch or two higher. Relax again and you will discover the sensation of a deep seat. It is the feeling of 'spreading your seat across the saddle'.

It is only when the rider and the instructor fully understand what a deep seat is that lungeing can be of value.

The use of the hand on the pommel can be of great value, but only when used with finger-tip pressure, not when used with force.

As well as being invaluable for developing balance and a deep seat, lungeing can be very helpful to those who have stiff shoulders and arms and all the related problems. Because riders are not using their reins, the arms and shoulders can be carefully observed. The arms should 'hang' down and dangle loosely, the knuckles bouncing a little. The arms should not be held down. As long as any problems relating to balance have been dealt with there are some exercises which can help these arm tension problems.

SIMPLE EXERCISES

Work first in walk, then in sitting or rising trot, and ultimately (some months later) in canter.

☐ Check that your body is upright and your head held correctly, then raise your arms forward, to shoulder height. Let them drop down with their own weight. They should swing loosely until they come to rest. Repeat until your arms and shoulders feel totally relaxed.

☐ Hold your hands in the normal riding position and then straighten both arms as if offering two cups of tea. Repeat smoothly several times (without spilling the tea). Experience the movement of your shoulder blades.

☐ Shrug your shoulders upwards and force them higher and higher. When they become painful, relax. They are now in the correct position for riding.

☐ Now hold your arms sideways but only half-way to shoulder height, with the palms facing forward. Keep your head up and experience this wonderful 'open-chested' feeling. Imagine yourself sunbathing. This is very helpful in relaxing the shoulders and relieving arm tensions.

The rider's aims at all times should be:

- Balance.
- Straightness.
- Suppleness.
- No gripping or clutching with legs.
- Relaxed seat muscles.
- Head up and eyes looking forward.
- Toes held just above heels but without force or ankle stiffness.
- Loose arms and 'heavy shoulders'.

Without force or stress try to:

- Increase the controlled mobility of the hip joint and spine.
- Bring the knee farther back and lower.
- Develop a lasting and equal contact of the lower leg which breathes with the horse's sides.
- Harmonise completely with the movements of the horse.

CHAPTER

17

Rider Position Faults

Understanding your own faults is half way to achieving success. Knowing the feel of the correction that is needed and what it feels like is three-quarters of the way there.

It is very difficult to achieve this by yourself, with no one to tell you 'Yes, you've got it right!' I hope that the notes on the following pages will help in this seemingly endless quest for the ideal. In your struggles, remember that though 'classical' is frequently talked about and envied, most of us – because of our physiques – have to make some compromises. As long as a compromise does not affect the horse in any way it has to be the best solution. It is certainly far better than looking good but being ineffectual and giving your horse all the wrong messages.

I have endeavoured to explain in the following sections that faults are seldom what they may at first appear to be. It is essential for both riders and instructors to seek the root cause of any problem. Superficial corrections have no lasting value.

When he teaches, the instructor must experiment with words, until something he says 'clicks' in the rider's mind. He must use images and stretch his own imagination to its fullest extent. He must never be afraid to say, 'No, that's not the problem, let's try something else.'

Only one fault should be dealt with at a time, so the instructor's ability to assess the fundamental problem is important. Praise is also a vital ingredient, for the rider learns what to do only by discovering which feelings to re-create.

Every problem has a key. Between the instructor and the pupil the right one must be found. The door will then open.

FAULTS RELATED TO BALANCE

BEHIND THE MOVEMENT IN RISING TROT

Apparent Fault

The rider is clearly seen to drop behind the movement as he returns to the saddle, landing with a thump and a fraction too soon, and therefore not being exactly in rhythm with the horse's trot. He may also straighten his hip and knee joints in an attempt to keep himself out of the saddle until the moment of return: though gravity usually takes over before this. The difficulty can also be accompanied by the rider gripping up with his knees and lower legs in an attempt to get himself out of the saddle again. Inevitably the hands are far from independent and either go up and down with the rider's body or are pressed down on the neck in an attempt to find stability.

This fault is more frequently noted among tall riders with long thighs and long upper bodies, often because they are afraid to incline their shoulders forward enough to remain in balance.

Because of this fault the horse often stiffens his back, loses balance, and hurries.

Cause

The rider has not learned to change his centre of gravity as he rises from his seat bones to the balls of his feet. Because of this, he is pushing himself out of the saddle instead of allowing the horse to move him forwards and upwards.

Correction

The rider must find his own centre of gravity. *There is no classical position in rising trot*. His task is solely to remain in balance and to return to the saddle softly and in harmony with the horse. Read *Chapter 8 (The Rising Trot)*. The movement *must* be felt as a forward and downward motion, not the frequently taught 'up – down'.

Recommended Exercises

The rider should establish his own ideal position at the halt. He should be careful not to stick his bottom out but should try instead to keep his hip and knee joints bent, in order to bring the hips further forward over the balls of the feet. He should be able to do this without a contact with the reins, and once he has established what he thinks is his 'rising trot

96

position', he should be able to move his arms about with ease. (The independent seat.)

He should now try the same thing at the walk, then finally at the trot, holding the position without returning to the saddle. Once this becomes easy he can progress to the normal rising trot. He should feel that if there happened to be a drawing pin on the saddle he could raise himself immediately. This will ensure that he does not flop back clumsily into the saddle.

I also suggest to riders that they should lower themselves into the saddle like Queen Victoria into a chair proffered by a footman. Assume that the chair is still there, but be ready to raise yourself just in case the footman has not accomplished his task.

In her book *Centred Riding* Sally Swift suggests that the rider should imagine that his feet are on the ground. I think this is particularly helpful if you also imagine getting up from a chair with your feet well underneath you.

A useful exercise is to change diagonals every fourth 'rise' by holding the rising position for an extra beat instead of sitting for that beat. This is very much more difficult than it sounds. If you can do it correctly and fluently you are certainly well in balance for rising trot. It is a good way to start your first trot of the day.

PHYSICAL EXERCISES
1. All *Balancing Exercises* and the *Hip Suppling Exercise* of squatting.

2. Raising and lowering yourself from a hard chair. Be sure to keep your back flat and your weight well distributed over your feet, not merely into the heels (which makes your bottom stick out).

DOUBLE BOUNCE IN RISING TROT

Apparent Fault
The rider makes a double bump in the saddle each time he returns to it.

Cause
A lack of balance, being behind the movement. This causes the rider to return to the saddle too soon and in front of the rhythm.

Correction
As for: *Behind the Movement in Rising Trot.*

97

As for: *Behind the Movement in Rising Trot.*

IN FRONT OF THE MOVEMENT IN RISING TROT

Apparent Fault

The rider leans forward when his seat is in the saddle. He is rather collapsed in his waist yet his rounded back is stiff and because he has to push himself out of the saddle, great strain is put on his legs and lower back. This creates stiffness and his body is unable to absorb the movement of the rise and sit. His head is generally bent back causing tension in the upper spine and between the shoulder blades. He will certainly be gripping with his legs, rather like a monkey, and probably supporting himself on his hands too. He may clutch at the reins and probably feel his toes curling under in his boots.

When he rises, he may spring upwards like a jack-in-the-box, opening the hip and knee angles wide, only to collapse again – virtually on to the horse's neck. Conversely, he may barely rise, because of the effort required, returning to his collapsed position well ahead of the correct moment, thus causing an 'extra' bump in the saddle. The rider will then become exceedingly tired.

This fault can be sustained in the more experienced rider if the tendency has not been corrected. Riders who have 'ridden all their lives' without proper tuition often retain early habits, and they are difficult to lose.

Cause

This fault tends to occur in the novice rider who has not yet fully come to terms with the rhythmic movement of the horse, and certainly not with the irregular movements which it makes.

He uses strength in place of skill and has yet to discover his own changing centre of gravity.

Anxiety probably plays a large part in this problem. It is a natural instinct to lower your centre of gravity when difficulties occur. For anyone threatened by speed or awkward movements leaning forward is a natural reaction. We would rather fall on our faces with our hands and arms flung out to save and protect us, than fall on our backs.

Lack of muscle tone, incorrect reflexes and insufficient co-ordination are also contributing factors.

Correction

The same as for *Behind the Movement in Rising Trot*. Once the rider is in balance he will not resort to the above contortions. His muscles will stop aching and a happy smile will appear on his face.

It is important for him to develop the feel of sitting tall, and to bear the following points in mind:

☐ The feel of being a puppet supported by a solitary string fastened to the centre of the top of his head (*Chapter 6*). His spine will then support him instead of dragging him, with a collapsing waist, towards the ground.

☐ That the movement, as he rises, is similar to getting up from a hard chair and stepping forward to greet someone, looking them straight in the eye.

☐ That the rising trot is forwards, not upwards.

Recommended Exercises

ON THE LUNGE

Anxiety is the principal problem to be overcome. Plenty of work at walk on a quiet lunge horse will help. In the early stages the rider should try, if possible, not to hold on to the saddle or to a neck strap, as this will distort his ability to find his own balance. It is better by far to develop confidence first at walk.

☐ In order to overcome initial anxiety, any light-hearted exercises on the lunge at halt or walk will be of benefit. Moving around in the saddle will establish that you do not fall off if you shift a little to either side or lean backwards and forwards. Any loosening movements will do, such as arm swinging, body turning, leg swinging and toe touching.

☐ Again, working on the lunge, without reins, use the 'open-chested' exercise already suggested in *Lungeing the Rider*. The rider should learn to enjoy the 'open-chested' feeling: not of pressing his shoulder blades back but of lifting his face to the sun.

PHYSICAL EXERCISES

The purpose of the following is to improve general rider body-tone.
The full range of *Balancing Exercises*.
The full range of *Spine Mobility Exercises*.
The *Hip Mobility Exercises* BUT NOT 4.
The full range of *Leg and Foot Exercises*.

This will be enough for the time being.

THE FORK SEAT

Apparent Fault

The rider seems to be tilted on to his pubic arch and, through hollowing his back, looks *very* upright and stiff. His lower legs either stick out from the horse's sides or are too far back.

In motion the rider will show a good deal of body movement because of the general stiffness of his position.

Cause

The rider is not sitting on the correct part of his seat bones. Instead, he is

Left *The fork seat. The rider is sitting on her fork and not sufficiently on her seat bones.*

Right *The collapsed seat. The rider is sitting on the back edge of the seat bones with a collapsed back.*

on the front edge of them and therefore taking the weight principally on to his thighs. The top of the rider's hip bones are not in line with his hip joint and shoulder, but are tilted in front. In an attempt to keep upright he hollows his back. Tension can be the root cause of this fault if the seat muscles are tightened, but, even more fundamentally, the rider is probably not in balance.

Correction
The only way to put this right is to sit on the correct part of the seat bones. Discovering *exactly* the right spot on which to sit will give the rider an everlasting point of reference and is one of the most important principles of riding. The seat bones are the rider's 'foundation stone'. From them his legs grow downwards and his body upwards. The legs are like roots seeking moisture deep in the earth, while the body is like a tree growing up towards the light.

The seat bones must sit in the lowest part of the saddle and the rider must find his centre of gravity and place his body above them in perfect balance. He should feel that even if his legs were cut off he could still sit there.

The best way to discover the individual 'spot' is by raising the knees as already described in *Chapter 6*.

Once this position is discovered, tension and stiffness usually disappear. The rider should think of his spine as a stack of building blocks neatly arranged one on top of the other, not built in a weak curve.

Recommended Exercises
Spine Mobility (2) and *(4)*.
Hip Mobility (1), (3) and *(6)*.

THE COLLAPSED SEAT

Apparent Fault
The rider has a rounded back and his seat is tucked underneath him. He seems limply over-relaxed. His heels are usually above his toes. His legs also look ineffectual and slack. His hands may be resting on the horse's neck.

Cause
He is sitting on the back edge of his seat bones with the top of his hip bones behind the line formed by his hip joint and shoulder.

This type of rider probably sits with his elbows on the table, walks with rounded shoulders, and enjoys flopping into a comfortable armchair. His muscle tone is poor, so he finds it an effort to support his own body in an upright way.

Correction

First the rider must change his basic posture when off the horse, so that his body gets used to holding itself up. He must exercise to help build muscle. Once he is in better physical order the position correction is exactly the same as for a *fork seat* (page 101).

This is a chicken and egg situation. The rider is collapsed because it is too much effort to sit up. If he could first make the effort to sit up he would get stronger, and soon no effort would be required.

Recommended Exercises

Walking and sitting in an upright manner.
Swimming.
The full range of *Balancing Exercises*.
Spine Mobility (1), (2) and *(4)*.
Hip Mobility (1), (2), (3), (6).
Shoulders and Arms.
Regular work on a lunge rein. The 'open-chested' exercise on page 94 will give the rider with the collapsed seat the best insight into the feeling of 'sitting up' correctly. Being lunged in sitting trot and canter in this position will accomplish much.

IN FRONT OF THE MOVEMENT (AT OTHER PACES)

Apparent Fault

This fault can appear in all or any of the paces, as well as at the rising trot, already explained.

IN WALK the rider's shoulders are slightly in front of the vertical line: ear-shoulder-hip-heel. His back will not move freely. He may grip upwards.

IN SITTING TROT, again, his shoulders are in front of the vertical line. This time the stiffness in his back has worse effects, for it means that he is unable to absorb the movement of the trot. He will therefore be seen to bounce or bump uncomfortably. He will probably stiffen or tense his arms and grip with his legs. In extreme cases the toe will be lower than the heel.

IN CANTER he swings forward but his shoulders never come reciprocally

In front of the movement. Tipping forward is a common fault in the anxious rider.

far enough back. As a result his seat does not stay close to the saddle but is bounced out as the first hind leg of the canter sequence comes into the air during the moment of suspension.

Cause

By not sitting upright the rider is not on his seat bones. He is fixing his hips or only allowing them forward movement. He is 'blocking' reciprocal backwards movement. Most particularly he is stopping the ripple of movement that should continue through his spine. This problem can stem from anxiety.

Correction

Find the correct position on the seat bones and allow the pelvis and spine to move equally backwards and forwards on either side of this central position. The rider should imagine that his seat bones are golf balls on which he rocks to and fro. To understand fully the correct movement required read *Chapter 7, 8,* or *9,* depending upon the pace. The movement of the horse must go right through the rider's hip joints and spine and not be blocked at any point by stiffening.

It is quite possible that the rider will at first feel that he is leaning backwards: sometimes even before he has reached a vertical position. It must be understood that it is a quite normal sensation when related to this particular problem.

Recommended Exercises
Of prime value will be exercises on the lunge without reins. Work with arms held sideways at shoulder height, then with arms partly raised sideways, palms facing forwards. Both these exercises will encourage the rider to find his correct balance and to open his chest.
Spine Mobility Exercises (1), (2), and *(4).*
Hip Mobility Exercises (1), (3), and *(6).*

LOWER LEG TOO FAR BACK

Apparent Fault
The lower leg is carried too far back all the time, with the heel sometimes above the level of the toes.

Cause
The rider is probably in front of the movement. He may have too much weight on the ball of his foot.

Correction
See *Behind the Movement.*

The rider must find the right balance between the weight in the stirrup iron on the ball of his foot and the weight in his heel. More weight into the heel will usually correct this mistake if it is not otherwise related to a fundamentally poor balance.

Recommended Exercises
Full range of *Balancing Exercises.*
Ankle Exercises.

BEHIND THE MOVEMENT (AT OTHER PACES)

Apparent Fault
The rider's shoulders come behind the vertical line and the head usually tips forward. Sometimes the lower legs come forward. The back may be rounded or hollowed, as well.

Lower leg too far back.

Behind the movement. Commonly seen in rising trot, canter and as the rider returns to the saddle in rising trot.

☐ This is a rather sophisticated fault not infrequently seen in international dressage arenas.

☐ As a seat aid momentarily applied, being a fraction behind the vertical is acceptable, sustained it is not.

☐ The fault is sometimes noticeable in sitting trot, especially in medium and extended trot. It must be understood that while it is an effective driving aid, its prolonged use will stiffen most horses' backs. Though very strong horses with lightweight riders are able to retain their natural swing despite the persistent use of this faulty position, it cannot be commended in classical riding.

Cause
The position is probably 'intended'. If not, it may be caused by stiff hips

and back, or weak back muscles. The rider will certainly be sitting on the back edge of his seat bones.

Correction

Find the correct position on the seat bones. Lengthen the distance between the waist and the chest, and bring the ear in line with the shoulder.

Make sure that the back is being used correctly and that the spine and hip joints are moving reciprocally.

Recommended Exercises

For the strong rider who has developed the habit, lungeing without stirrups is recommended.

If the fault is due to weakness or lack of mobility the full range of *Spine and Hip Mobility Exercises*.

The 'cat' stretching exercise (*Spine Mobility 1*) can be extended to raising the leg out behind (though previously NOT recommended) because in this instance the back needs more strength.

SITTING TOO FAR BACK IN THE SADDLE. THE 'CHAIR' SEAT

Apparent Fault

The rider is sitting a long way back in the saddle. His seat is too close to the cantle. His back is sometimes rounded. His legs are usually too far forward. He sometimes leans forward. In rising trot he is always behind the movement.

Cause

The saddle.

The saddle must fit both the horse and the rider. If it is too high in front – because it is a little too narrow for the horse – or too low behind – through lack of stuffing – the lowest part will inevitably be too far back. Naturally enough, the rider's seat will slide to the lowest part and unless his feet reach forward to the stirrup irons he will not be able to keep the leathers straight.

Correction

For immediate help, put a thick pad under the back of the saddle.

If the fault is due to lack of stuffing, take it to the saddler.

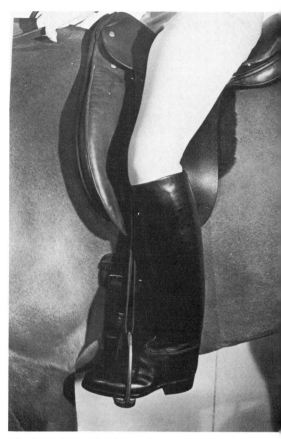

The chair seat. The rider is sitting upright but on the back of the seat bones, with the lower legs stuck forward. This is sometimes accompanied by forced-down heels.

The lower leg too far forward (note that the stirrup leather is not at right angles to the ground).

Unfortunately the problem is more frequently caused by a saddle that is too narrow for the horse or the wrong shape for the rider.

When the saddle is at fault it is impossible for the rider to correct his position. Children are most likely to suffer from this when their ponies get 'summer' fat, and what was a nicely fitting saddle becomes too narrow.

RISING TOO HIGH

Apparent Fault

In rising trot the rider rises too far from the saddle, straightening his knee and hip joints. As he comes into the upright position he pushes his hips forwards, almost with a jerk. He sometimes uses the weight of his returning seat as a powerful driving aid. This can stiffen the horse and cause him to hollow his back.

Cause

The rider has not found his balance during the actual rising moment and the returning moment. It is rather like someone jumping to his feet and dropping back again. He could not make the movement slowly at the halt.

The rider is probably perfectly in balance at the actual peak of the rise: almost, in fact, like someone standing to attention.

Correction and Recommended Exercises

The same as for *Behind the Movement in Rising Trot*.

18

Faults Related to Crookedness

This group of faults is the most difficult to cure: principally because the rider *feels* straight and any correction that he makes actually seems to him as though he is putting himself in a contorted position.

I strongly believe that unless crookedness is due to a physical imbalance which the rider was born with; to unequal muscular development; or to injury, the fault is *caused entirely by the rider being behind the movement or otherwise out of balance.*

It is very important to consider which category the rider's problem falls into. Has he:

Been born out of shape?

Become out of shape?

Or:

Does he lack balance?

In order to determine the cause it is better to appraise the rider while he is standing on his feet. For self-correction look in a mirror.

The first category poses problems. Out-of-shape development can be brought about through injury and a habit of protection or through strong use of one side of the body as with, say, squash players.

Lack of balance relates to *Chapter 16.* In my opinion it incorporates the greater number of faults.

THE COLLAPSED HIP

Apparent Fault

This fault is very obvious when seen from behind the rider. His seat and weight are clearly more to one side of the saddle than the other, and in order to keep his balance he leans to the other side. Because of the seat displacement there is more weight in the stirrup, and the leg is long on the

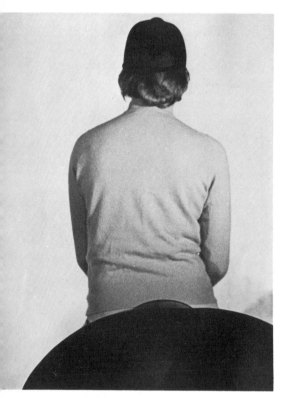

Collapsed right hip.

weighted side. On the leaning-in side there is little weight on the seat bone or in the stirrup, and the leg looks shorter, the heel sometimes coming above the toe.

Because the rider is leaning, one shoulder is lower than the other.

This fault can be observed from the side, and if a rider is continually carrying the same shoulder in advance of the other on both reins, he may well be collapsing one hip. Unequal leg and hand positions can provide a further clue.

Cause

The rider's seat bones are unequally weighted and placed more to one side of the saddle than the other. Generally the fault develops through unequal co-ordination of the body. Those who are right-handed have better co-ordination on their right sides.

The more confirmed this fault, the more difficult it is to eradicate.

I do not want to provide an escape route for riders, but must mention that a horse who is particularly stiff on one rein can sometimes produce 'crookedness' in any rider.

110

Correction

At the halt the rider should place his seat bones equally on either side of an imaginary centre line drawn through the saddle. He must feel equal weight on them and on his stirrup irons. He will need help in establishing this position, as it will feel unnatural and strange. Raising himself and returning squarely to the saddle at the halt will help him to establish the position.

The sensation of lengthening the weak side of his body – so that his leg feels heavier and weighted on that side – can help.

This is a fault that the rider will find very hard to correct himself, as he will feel straight even though he is crooked. He will need constant help and encouragement.

Recommended Exercises

These can be exceptionally helpful in developing the weak side of the body, as long as they are only practised on the side of the body that is weak.

It is essential to understand that the fundamental problem is a lack of co-ordination on that particular side and that better nerve routes to and from the brain must be developed. This is accomplished by repetition.

The full range of *Balancing Exercises*.

Kneel on the floor as for *Spine Mobility (1)*. Lift the leg on the weak side, and straighten it out behind you, raising it as high as possible without twisting your body. Then draw the knee up to your chin. Repeat.

Hip Mobility (1) and *(2)* only on the weak side, *(6)* on both sides.

Legs and Feet (1) and *(2)*.

Legs and Feet (3) with the weak leg only.

Fingers with emphasis on the weak hand.

Shoulders and Arms with the weak arm only.

ONE HIP IN ADVANCE OF THE OTHER

Apparent Fault

Riders have to be seen from both sides before this fault can be diagnosed. The shoulder is generally drawn back on the same side as the hip is back. The lower leg on that side is often in a good position. The leg on the other side is forward and off the girth. Any unequal holding of the legs – such as one toe out and one toe straight – can be attributed to the same cause. A twist in rising trot can sometimes also be traced to this problem.

It is difficult visually to relate this fault to the hips unless the angle of

111

Crookedness due to the right hip being in advance of the left.

incorrectness is very pronounced. The fault is usually more obvious and more exaggerated when the rider's backward hip is on the outside of turns or circles.

Cause

The seat bones are not square and equally weighted in the saddle. This may be due to weakness on the side of the body that is lagging behind, or to a stiff horse.

Correction

The weight must be felt equally on both seat bones and the faulty hip must be consciously pushed forward. When using the influence of the weight on the inside seat bone as an aid, the rider must be careful to lengthen his leg on that side. Some aids do require the slight advancing of one hip. This must not be confused with the sustained error of one hip permanently being held in front of the other. As soon as the hip is corrected the crooked shoulders and unequal legs will straighten.

Recommended Exercises

As for *The Collapsed Hip on the Weak Side*.

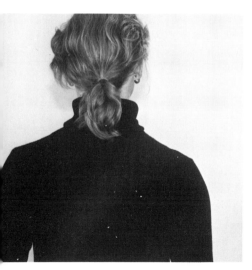

This rider is naturally crooked and only remedial medical treatment could be expected to show any improvement.

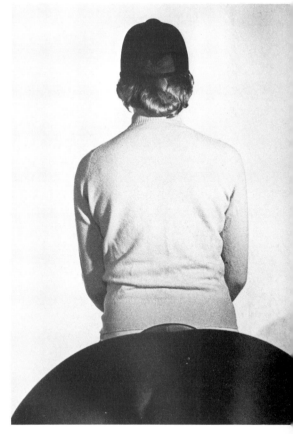

Sitting squarely. No rider is absolutely symmetrical and this rider is as straight as she can be.

ONE SHOULDER DROPPED

Apparent Fault
The rider has one shoulder lower than the other.

Cause
Check that the fault is not in fact caused by the rider collapsing one hip or leaving one hip behind.

It is frequently caused by a physical irregularity, or to a deformity relating to curvature of the spine.

The rider may be collapsing his waist on the dropped side, or very tense and stiff on the raised side. If there is tension it may well be caused by riding a horse that takes a very strong contact on one rein and practically none on the other. It may be that strength or tension is being offered by one side of the body to compensate for weakness on the other.

113

Correction

If there is a deformity, medical help should be sought. If nothing can be done, then treat it as for a physical defect. If you are riding competitively, wear additional padding on the relevant shoulder of your jacket.

If the waist is collapsed it will usually be to the inside that the rider's shoulder drops, possibly on both reins. He should be conscious of making the distance between the top of his hip bone and his armpit equal on both sides and should feel equal weight in both seat bones.

If the problem is produced by tension on the raised side, riding another horse will probably give an indication for diagnostic purposes. But the rider should be careful not to pass on his stiffness to another horse. This can – and frequently does – happen.

The rider should try to imagine that he has a hand pressing down on both his shoulders, with his spine being drawn up between them by his head.

Recommended Exercises

For a collapsed waist, use the same strengthening exercises as for a collapsed hip on the collapsed side. *Spine Mobility (1)* is excellent with the additional leg movement, but only on the weak side. The aim is to develop equal support for the body from the muscles.

Lungeing is also excellent.

RISING CROOKEDLY

Apparent Fault

As the rider moves up and down in rising trot his body twists and one shoulder draws back. As he sits, he straightens again. Whichever rein he rides on the same shoulder comes back, but it is generally more pronounced when the shoulder coming back is on the opposite side to the turn or circle.

Cause

The rider is probably behind the movement and making too much effort to get himself out of the saddle. One hip may be held back. See *One Hip in Advance of the Other.*

Due to weakness on one side of his body, the strong side initiates the movement and pulls the weak side up after it with consequent 'twisting'.

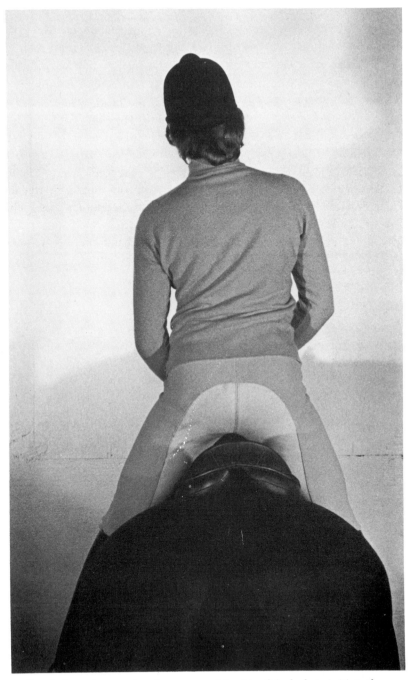

Crookedness due to using the stronger right side of the body to initiate the movement of leaving the saddle (right seat bone leaving the saddle first).

Correction

The rider should check that his rising trot is 'in balance'. See *Behind the Movement in Rising Trot*. This may well provide an instant cure. I personally have dealt with this problem with a very athletic, physically strong young rider who was very 'crooked' indeed. He persistently rose off his right seat bone, and I realised that this was because he was a squash and tennis player. Nothing I said improved him until I thought of checking his balance in rising trot. He was just slightly behind the movement. Once this was corrected, the twist was eradicated as if by magic. Because he was so strong he did not appear to be behind the movement.

Once in balance, the rider must make sure that both his seat bones leave the saddle and return to it at exactly the same moment.

Recommended Exercises

As for *Behind the Movement in Rising Trot*.
If for weakness on one side only: as *The Collapsed Hip* on the weak side only.

TWISTING IN CANTER

Apparent Fault

The rider twists at the waist on each stride of canter. One shoulder persistently comes back and the other forward.

Cause

The rider may be semi-standing in his stirrups.

The horse may be hanging on one rein.

The rider is certainly not keeping equal weight throughout on his seat bones. Instead of allowing the movement to be absorbed as a to and fro action of the hips, spine and upper body, he is absorbing it in a sideways manner.

Correction

To help find the feel of the movement, work with short stirrups in the forward seat. As the upper body learns only to move backwards and forwards balanced on the balls of the feet, the rider can softly bring himself into the saddle and re-create the same feeling as a soft to and fro in the saddle. He must be careful not to tense on one side of his back

116

muscles nor tighten his buttocks. This fault is more a bad habit than anything else.

Recommended Exercises
Balancing Exercises.
Spine Mobility Exercises (1) and *(4)*.
Hip Mobility Exercises (4) and *(6)*.

THE STIFF HORSE

Apparent Fault
With good riders it is hard to see or to be aware of very slight inadequacies in the weight distribution, but the horse most certainly will inform you of them.

When a horse apparently does not respond to the rider's inside leg aid by bending correctly on one rein, it is frequently the rider's fault. He weights the outside more than the inside seat bone and stirrup.

Sometimes the rider resorts to trying to 'hold the horse out' with his hands – even raising the inside hand and pushing it against the horse's neck by crossing it over the withers, or pulling with the outside rein.

Cause
On turns, corners and circles, centrifugal force naturally moves the rider to the outside of the saddle. The stiffer the horse the more the rider tends to be moved to the outside of the saddle.

This usually happens on the rider's least co-ordinated side: probably his left. Horses are more predominantly stiff to the left.

As the rider is moved to the outside of the saddle the weight goes off his inside seat bone and lightens the weight in the inside stirrup.

Correction
The rider must lengthen rather than shorten the side of his body that is unweighted. The corrections are the same as for *Collapsed Hip*.

He should put more weight into the inside stirrup and on to the inside seat bone.

Recommended Exercises
As for *Collapsed Hip*.

See picture on next page.

One hand held out, the other crossing the withers.

ADDITIONAL FAULTS

The following faults are frequently observed in riders but are not necessarily attributed to their fundamental causes.

Fault

Gripping upwards on one side.

Suggested remedy: read *Collapsed Hip, One Hip in Advance of the Other* and *The Stiff Horse.*

Faults

(a) Head held crookedly.

(b) Unequal hand positions.

These can both be related to a variety of more fundamental crookedness problems and all the preceding chapters on crookedness should be read.

Practically any unequalness in any part of the body, unless due to physical abnormality, can be related to the fundamental misplacement of the seat bones or lack of balance.

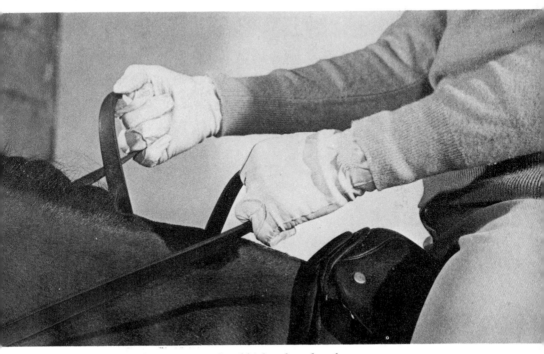

Unequal hand positions: one hand higher than the other.

119

Gripping up.

19

Faults Caused by Tension

That much-used cliché 'relax' is the most over-used riding instruction of all.

To some extent I have already described and explained how muscles, tendons and ligaments are used. Perhaps here it is necessary really to appreciate just how our muscles function *for* and *against* us.

Without muscles we would collapse totally and would be unable to move. Every muscle in our body is always in partial use, even during sleep.

☐ Muscles are made up of many small bundles of fibres. At rest the muscle uses a few fibres at maximum strength. As more effort is required of the muscle, so more fibres are brought into use at maximum strength.

☐ A muscle works only by contraction, it cannot push. It can be used in three ways:

(1) As a 'prime mover' a muscle initiates the movement so for example if you hollow your back the back muscles contract.

(2) As an 'antagonistic' when muscle supports the movement and controls it. In the case of the hollowing back, the muscles on the front of the body are playing this supporting role. If they did not do so the back would hollow uncontrollably, probably with a jerk, the shoulders and head straining back until you ended up by falling over.

(3) As 'fixators' muscles generally work as a group, though they can work singly. When operating as fixators they are 'holding' muscles and come into use when, for example, you point your finger, hold your leg out, or raise and straighten your arms. They are also used in this way to control the shoulder, which is an unstable joint reliant on muscle to hold it in position.

☐ The rider is said to be tense when he uses more fibres than necessary with both the 'prime movers' and the 'antagonistics': i.e. one muscle using its strength against another.

☐ He is also tense if his muscles are rather weak and the 'fixators' do more than hold, instead, stiffening and becoming rigid. This is frequently noticeable in the shoulder.

When the rider is out of balance he has to use his muscles very strongly. This is frequently where tension problems begin.

☐ A tense – or even very strong – rider can stiffen his horse's back and ruin his paces by 'blocking' the natural movement. The rider must always be conscious of letting the movement of the horse flow between his legs, seat and back. The horse's energy must be like the continuous movement of a wide river, not like the pressurised water in a hosepipe. If the energy is forced through the rider's legs, seat and back it will lack suppleness and fluency.

OVERALL TENSION

Apparent Fault
The rider is unnecessarily tense and tight. He frequently holds his breath.

Cause
Fear, worry, anxiety or trying too hard. A nervous disposition.
This is a mental rather than a physical problem.

Correction
Confidence which comes with time is the ultimate cure. But learning to control tension is possible through a full range of Yoga relaxation exercises particularly when they include correct breathing.

It sometimes helps this type of rider to talk to his horse or to hum a tune. His own voice and pitch will tell him when he is reaching an anxiety peak.

Recommended Exercises
Read a book on Yoga, and follow the instructions.
Breathing Exercises.
All the Recommended Exercises, except those for arms, will help to develop control and enhance suppleness.

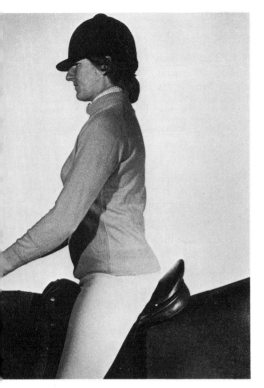

Back tension: a stiff, hollow back has brought the shoulders forward.

Hip tension: stiff arms (above) are sometimes caused by stiff hips.

BACK AND HIP TENSION
Apparent Fault
This fundamental fault can show in almost any part of the rider's body.

The rider may bump in the saddle and sit against the movement of the horse.

He may tip forwards or backwards.

His shoulders may stiffen and his arms may correspondingly straighten or tense up.

His legs may stick forwards or outwards.

Nearly all rider faults are traceable to this basic problem of tension. It can be the root cause of almost anything.

Cause
Probably lack of balance; pain; injury; or anxiety. The rider tenses up or holds his back muscles in a futile attempt to stay 'with' or on the horse.

123

Correction

The rider must first find his centre of gravity in all paces and must fully understand the movements that he should be making. He must learn the feel of the rhythm of the pace and must let his body flow with it. The pelvis must initiate any movement, and the back must allow it to ripple through.

Read and understand *Chapters 6 to 11*.

Recommended Exercises

The full range of *Balancing Exercises*.
The full range of *Hip and Back Mobility Exercises*.
Lungeing at a slow trot will also help.

TIGHT SEAT MUSCLES

Apparent Fault

The rider's seat lacks 'depth'.

Cause

This is a common and major problem, probably caused by mental tension.

The rider is contracting his seat muscles and forcing muscle tissue between his seat bones and the saddle. At the same time the rider generally tenses his thighs. It is difficult to do one without the other.

This may be caused by stirrup leathers which are too long. The rider therefore reaches his toes down and pinches his thighs – and thus his seat muscles – together.

Correction

To understand this fault the rider should first sit upright on a hard chair and squeeze his buttocks together; without changing his posture he should then relax them. He will feel his body lowering by inches.

Once in the saddle the rider must attempt the same degree of relaxation in all paces.

Breathing out is also helpful, as long as the rider does not collapse his waist, which has the effect of lowering his centre of gravity. It is very important to do this correctly. (See *Breathing Exercises*.)

The rider must, of course, sit up correctly. With his back correctly balanced, he should then try to imagine that the base of his spine is being drawn downwards through the saddle by a heavy weight, his buttocks spreading themselves across the saddle. It is most important for the rider

Tight seat muscles. When the rider was asked to tighten her seat muscles her knee stiffened and her lower leg came forward.

Tight seat muscles causing a hollow back.

not to contract his seat muscles when using the back or weight aids. There is frequent confusion between seat muscle contraction and the correct movement and influence of the hips and spine.

Recommended Exercises
Breathing Exercises.

125

TIGHT THIGHS

Apparent Fault
The knee grips tightly against the saddle, and the lower leg is forced away from the horse's sides, usually with the toes turned out and the inner part of the foot lower than the outer. There may also be an apparent stiffness in the hips and back.

Cause
Possibly lack of balance, the rider attempting to hold on with a tight grip. (He may have been taught to grip with his knees.)

Tight seat muscles are a frequent cause (see page 124). Because of a lack of suppleness in the hip and back the rider is unable to balance.

This can also be due to the rider bringing his knee too far back under his hip and creating a sort of pinching upwards, allied to the 'fork seat'.

Correction
When the rider is able to move his hip joints and spine correctly he will feel so comfortably balanced that there will be no need to hold on with his legs.

If the rider is *forcing* the movement of his back rather than initiating it by tipping his pelvis forward and back he will be over-mobile in the saddle and doing a sort of 'belly dance'.

He must think about his knees being soft, his lower legs caressing his horse's sides, and remaining 'long' with the toes pointing forward and the heels lower. He must be careful not to start gripping with the back of his calves as an alternative.

If the rider is a novice this fault may take time to overcome. Balance comes partially through confidence, then the correct muscles have to be developed. But the rider should be made conscious of his fault so that he does not allow it to develop into a habit.

Recommended Exercises
Lungeing is excellent as long as it is carried out under careful supervision. There is a danger that the rider, if struggling, will hang on harder still. (Even off the lunge this is frequently the case with children when they are asked to work without stirrups. They clutch like mad with their legs and the whole exercise is counter productive.)

Full range of *Balancing Exercises.*

Full range of *Hip and Spine Mobility Exercises.*

The best exercises are the ones in which the legs are moved sideways and backwards.

GRIPPING WITH KNEES

Apparent Fault

The rider's knee is pressed into the saddle but his lower leg is held away from the horse's sides and his heel is pressed down too much. His toe may be turned outwards.

This position frequently brings the rider's seat out behind him and sometimes pushes his lower leg forwards.

Cause

The rider is probably (though not always) behind the movement. He is pushing his knee into the saddle and letting his weight drop heavily into

Gripping with the knees: the lower leg has been driven away from the horse's side by the tight knee.

127

his heel, probably with more weight on the inside of the stirrup iron.

He may have been taught to grip, and believes that it will hold him in the saddle.

Correction

First the rider must consciously loosen the inner thigh muscles (the adductors) allowing his lower leg to come softly against the horse's side. If his balance is not at fault this is all he will have to do.

The rider must take care not to put too much weight into his heel, as this will create greater tension in the calf and knee. He must keep his weight equally balanced between the ball of the foot and the heel. If balance is a problem he must then find his centre of gravity: in rising trot over the ball of the foot and the heel, in other paces correctly on his seat bones. He should sit in the central part of the saddle, not too far back. Above all he must retain the supple 'elastic' movement of his hips, knees, and ankles. These are a rider's shock absorbers and tightness in the knees and ankles will stop him using them.

Recommended Exercises

The *Balancing Exercises.*
The *Hip Mobility Exercises (2)* and *(5).*
The *Leg and Feet Exercises (1), (2),* and *(3).* DO NOT ON ANY ACCOUNT EXERCISE THE ANKLES OTHER THAN BY LETTING THEM HANG LOOSELY. They are already too strong and tense.

GRIPPING WITH BACKS OF CALVES

Apparent Fault

The rider's toes are turned out and the backs of his calves are constantly squeezing the horse's sides. This is most visible in rising trot when the rider squeezes every time he sits in the saddle.

Cause

Possibly lack of balance, the rider being behind the movement. See *Behind the Movement in Rising Trot.*

If only noticeable on one side, see *Collapsed Hip* and *One Hip in Advance of the Other.*

Generally this fault is caused by the rider trying to keep the contact of his lower legs; trying not to kick at the horse; or trying to use too much leg.

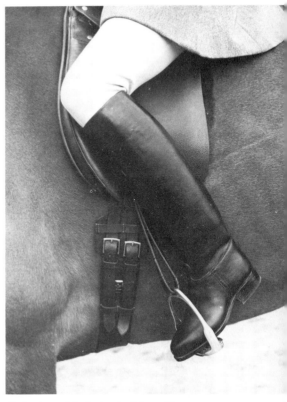

The lower leg has been driven away from the horse's side by the tight knee and too much weight on the inside of the stirrup iron, causing the rider to grip with the back of the calf.

Gripping with the back of the calf, sometimes termed gripping up. The rider clutches with the calves and the knees come up and forwards.

The problem more frequently occurs in riders with short legs.

Correction

The correct position and the correct leg aids can only be used when the rider has developed the right muscles. Read *Chapter 11*, and in particular *Chapter 15: Legs and Feet.*

The rider must learn to use his legs by closing them inwards with a soft knee, and with the contact of the lower leg coming softly against the horse's side.

This problem is further complicated if the rider has short legs and is riding a round-barrelled horse. As his knee will come above the widest part of the horse, he will either have to ride with a very loose knee – which with such conformation is almost impossible in rising trot – or he will have to shorten his stirrup leathers.

I think it was Seunig who suggested that the rider's legs should 'lie like wet flannels round the horse's sides'. When thinking of this helpful image the rider should be careful not to bend his ankle inwards.

Recommended Exercises
The whole range of *Leg and Feet Exercises*.
If sideways leg mobility is not good, *Hip Mobility Exercises* may also help.

HEELS TOO LOW

Apparent Fault
The rider's ankles are pushed down very deeply. Some people do not consider this a fault.

Cause
The rider may have very supple ankles, making it easier for him to let them drop deeply down rather than to maintain a reasonable amount of weight on the balls of his feet. The danger is that tension will be transferred to his whole lower leg, so that it will be difficult for him to keep a soft contact against his horse's sides.

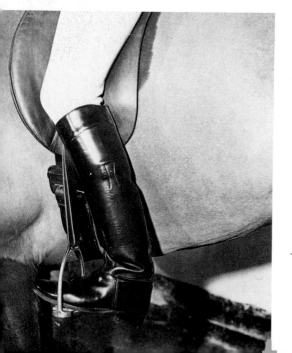

Heels too low: there is too much weight in the heel, which is being forced down too hard.

- ☐   The stirrup may often slip off his foot.

- ☐   He may also find it difficult to give good leg aids.

Correction

As for *Gripping with Knees*. Remember that anything forced creates tension. If the ankle is soft and supple and the weight spread between the ball of the foot and the heel there should be no problem, however deeply the heel goes down.

Recommended Exercises

Dancing, and discovering where he puts his weight: it should be on the balls of his feet or it will be hard luck on his poor partner, whether human or horse.

STIFF ANKLES

Apparent Fault

The rider's toe is below his heel.

Cause

As the cause may be gripping upwards, read *Chapter 17: Behind the*

Stiff ankle: the rider's toe is below his heel.

Movement, and also *Chapter 19: Gripping with Backs of Calves.* A common cause, however, is simply a lack of natural suppleness in the ankle. Women who frequently wear high heels often have this problem.

Correction
The rider must try to increase suppleness. This is not easy, as on a horse it must be done without force. For this particular fault it is essential to exercise *off the horse.*

Recommended Exercises
The full range of *Ankle Exercises.*
Without wearing shoes, repeatedly touch your toes with straight legs. Reach as far as possible, gradually extending the range without undue forcing.

TOES TURNED OUT

Apparent Fault
The rider's toes are turned outwards and the sole of his boot is sometimes visible from the side instead of being horizontal to the ground. His leg is drawn away from the horse's side.

Cause
☐ There may be lack of balance, tight knees or forced down ankles.

☐ More weight is being put on the inside of the stirrup than the outside. This twisted foot position causes the ankle to lose suppleness. If it is under tension, it ceases to act as a shock-absorber.

Correction
Check that the problem is not balance, tight knees, or forced down heels.
  Read *Chapter 8* again; also the preceding pages to this chapter.
  The rider must keep his little toe level with his big toe, without bending his ankle inwards. He must be careful not to curl his toes in his boots. At first it may help to exaggerate a little and to keep more weight on the outside edge of the stirrup.

Recommended Exercises
Hip Mobility Exercise (5).

CROOKED STIRRUP

Apparent Fault
The stirrup is not at right angles to the horse's body. It may be on the tip of the rider's toe.

Cause
One of the leg-related problems described in the preceding pages is probably the basic cause. If in one leg only, it is an indication of crookedness.

The rider is not feeling the weight of the stirrup equally across the ball of his foot.

Correction
Check *Balance*, *Gripping Up* and *Thigh and Knee Tightness*.

Crooked stirrup, usually caused by an unequal weight placement.

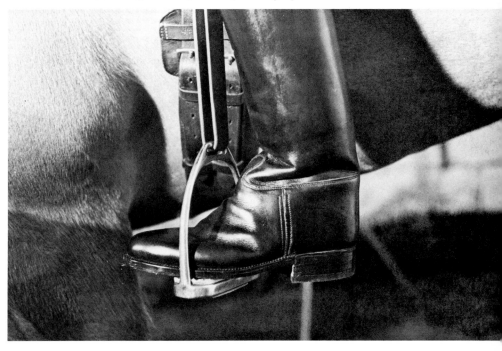

FOOT RIGHT HOME IN THE STIRRUP

Apparent Fault
The stirrup is right up against the heel of the rider's boot.

The rider's toe is sometimes down and his lower leg forward.

Cause
The rider is almost certainly 'behind the movement'. See *Chapter 16.*

The rider is probably 'gripping up'. See *Chapter 19.*

The leg is not stretched downwards and the weight is not being equally divided between the heel and the ball of the foot.

Correction
The rider must find his centre of gravity and let his legs grow downwards, the weight flowing through the ball of his foot towards his heel.

Almost certainly this is not an isolated problem and the root cause of balance and muscle tone must be fully explored.

STIFF SHOULDERS AND ARMS

Apparent Fault
Arms are straight or held still. There is tension across the rider's back. The shoulder blades and the shoulder and elbow joints do not move. The horse appears 'fixed' or resistant.

Cause
This very often stems from a lack of balance.

It can be caused by the rider's mental attitude to the carriage of his horse's head: i.e. that it must be held still and in position.

It may also be due to weakness in the rider's shoulders which makes the muscles fix in order to hold.

The rider may be trying too hard to keep a good contact. See also *Chapter 19: Hands Too Low.*

Correction
First find the correct balance in all paces. Then become aware of moving the shoulder blades, shoulder joints and elbow joints reciprocally.

Good breathing helps with all tension problems, especially those connected with the arms. Make sure the line elbow-hand-horse's mouth is maintained.

The arms should hang to the elbows like loose sleeves. The rider must be aware of the movement of the horse's head and the correct rein contact. Read *Chapter 12*.

The instructor should be able to observe recurrent wrinkles appearing between the rider's shoulder blades in rhythm with the movement of the horse.

Recommended Exercises
Full range of *Arm* and *Finger Exercises*.
Lungeing without reins is also excellent.

BOUNCING HANDS

Apparent Fault
The hands bounce up and down with the rider in sitting trot. Sometimes termed 'dancing hands'.

Cause
See *Unnecessary Movement*, page 140.

This can also be caused by the rider supporting his hands with the muscles of his forearm rather than the muscles of his upper arm. It causes general tension in the shoulder joints and 'fixes' the rider's arms in an inflexible way to his body.

Correction
If the rider concentrates on holding his hands up with his upper arms he will find that he is able to move his shoulders and therefore his arms quite independently.

Recommended Exercises
Lungeing. See *Exercises for Lungeing (1), (2), (3)* and *(4)*.

ELBOWS HELD OUT

Apparent Fault
The rider's elbows are held out and sometimes flap in rhythm with the horse's movement.

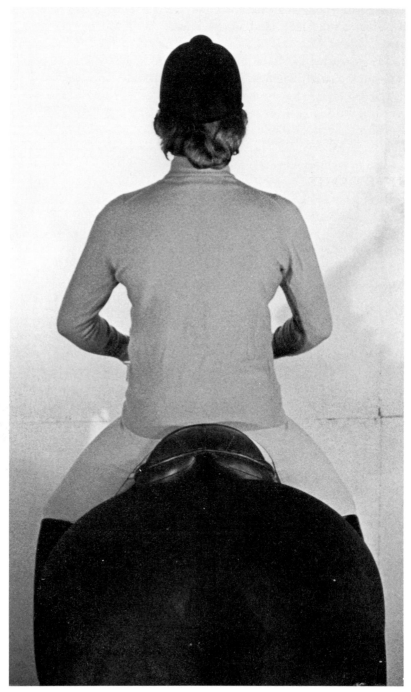

Elbows held out.

Cause
Tension in the back and shoulders.

Correction
See *Stiff Shoulders and Arms*, page 134.

Recommended Exercises
Lungeing without reins, arms hanging down.

STIFF WRISTS

Apparent Fault
The wrists are bent back, fixed, or held with the backs of the hands uppermost.

In some cases the wrists are rounded.

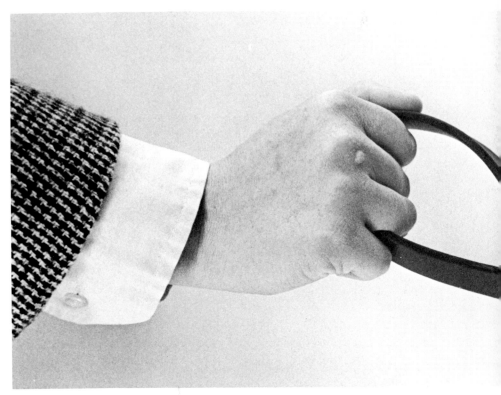

Stiff wrist: the wrist is bent back so that the straight line down the forearm is broken.

Cause

The stiffness may well be coming from fixed shoulders and elbows. If not, the rider is probably clenching his fists.

Correction

If the fault stems from the shoulders, the cure is as for *Stiff Shoulders*.

If the fists are clenched, the rider should let his hands hang down without reins just as he does when he is walking along. Then the fingers should be folded up and the arms raised to the riding position. The line of the arms should extend softly down the line of the backs of the hands.

When he feels this softer position, he can take up the reins again. (This should be done at the halt.)

When riding a difficult horse a rider often contorts his hand positions.

Recommended Exercises

The full range of *Wrist and Finger Exercises*.

Lungeing without reins with the hands dangling and in the riding position is also helpful.

A clenched fist. This produces tension in the arm and consequent stiffness.

Stiff neck: the chin is pulled back tightly, causing spine tension.

STIFF NECK

Apparent Fault

The rider is very still in his neck and there is obvious tension. He does not move or look about him. His jaw may also be clenched.

Cause

Usually: stiff shoulders.

Sometimes the neck itself is held rigid, which in turn can *make* the shoulders stiffen.

If the back is collapsed and weak the neck can become tense. See *Chapter 19*.

Correction

As for *Stiff Shoulders*.

If the neck itself is the problem, then looking calmly and frequently from left to right while riding can help. The head must be kept upright.

Recommended Exercises
The full range of *Spine Mobility Exercises*.
Head Rolling Round and Round. Shoulder Shrugging. Both to be carried out when dismounted.

TENSE JAW

Apparent Fault
The facial muscles look tense, especially round the jaw bone.

Cause
Determination or temper.

Correction
If determination is the cause, the rider should move his head about and talk. Determination is admirable but it must not turn into aggression. It is better to think positively about what has to be achieved rather than to grit your teeth which achieves nothing. If there is tension in the jaw there is probably a good deal of tension in other parts of the body.

Most people lose their tempers sometimes: generally just with themselves. If this happens, either get off and cool off, or have a walk and a think about the cause of your irritation.

Recommended Exercise
Deep-Breathing Exercise.

UNNECESSARY MOVEMENT

There are a number of faults which seem at first to be related to a lack of muscular control and which should therefore be regarded as belonging to the next chapter. They are in fact due to stiffness, despite the evidence of one part of the rider's body flopping about or bouncing in an uncontrolled way. For this reason I will deal with them here.

Apparent Fault
The rider's head, hands and arms, or legs move apparently involuntarily, despite the fact that his body seems to be in harmony with the horse. This fault is most frequently observed in sitting trot.

Cause

There is generally stiffness somewhere in the hip joints or spine.

The lack of movement in one part of the body causes too much movement in another. This is a whiplash type of movement. When you crack a whip, first of all your arm is loose. Then, to make the lash flick violently, it stiffens. So it is with a rider. If the flow of movement is briefly halted at some point, the end part of the body (head, hand, or leg) will flick. Sometimes the elbows join in.

Correction

It is useless to advise the rider to keep the offending part of his anatomy still: the more he tries, the more it will move. Keeping still on a horse in fact means moving with him, and if you try to stay still you become tense and are thrown about by the movement.

The first problem is to discover where the tension or stiffness lies. As it is probably only a small amount, anyway, it is better to work in the pace in which the problem shows up most. The rider should concentrate not on the problem, but on the rest of his body – especially the seat, hips and back area. He should feel the whole sensation of the movement, and should try to discover for himself just where there might be a little tension. It will be necessary to experiment with different ways of moving, and will probably be particularly helpful to think of the movement of the pelvis.

Recommended Exercises

Full range of *Spine Mobility* and *Hip Mobility Exercises*.

Lungeing will also help, because the rider will be able to concentrate fully on the feel of the correct movement.

CHAPTER
20

Faults Caused by Looseness

By the term 'loose' I do not mean 'supple'. I mean that the rider is floppy and lacks muscle tone.

The problems of looseness become faults of tension, for looseness in one part of the body becomes compensating tension in another. Even novice riders are rarely loose all over. Though they may lack co-ordination – and therefore control – over their limbs, in their efforts to succeed they frequently put considerable unnecessary strain on some muscles. This becomes tension.

Tired muscles (which are basically weak, and not up to the job) resort to tension and often 'fix' the joint.

With experienced riders there is a danger that parts of their bodies may become *too* strong, so they lose the fluency of a well-harmonised body. As a result, odd parts of their anatomy, such as head and hands, bounce about and become their weak links.

The aim of every rider should be to develop a fit, co-ordinated body, each part of which can carry out its normal function without resorting to another part for help.

If the rider's muscles are not strong enough to control the excessive movement of his joints it is quite possible to be over-supple. There is no more unattractive sight than that of a rider who 'belly dances' in the saddle because of an over-mobile spine. When we come to looseness, over-suppleness is not the greatest problem. It is far more likely to relate to lazy muscles and bad general habits.

As I have already said, there is not much point in the rider trying to sit well when he is on a horse if once back on his own feet he resorts to his sloppy habits and walks with round shoulders, head hanging, and stomach sagging. Good posture must become a habit, whether on or off the horse.

142

Collapsed waist.

COLLAPSED WAIST

Fault
The rider looks round-shouldered and rather slumped in the saddle. His back is rounded, his head often hangs down and his hands are too low. His legs often appear limp and ineffectual.

Cause
The rider is not sitting correctly on his seat bones. See *The Collapsed Seat*.

Correction
As for *Collapsed Seat*.

Recommended Exercises
As for *Collapsed Seat*.

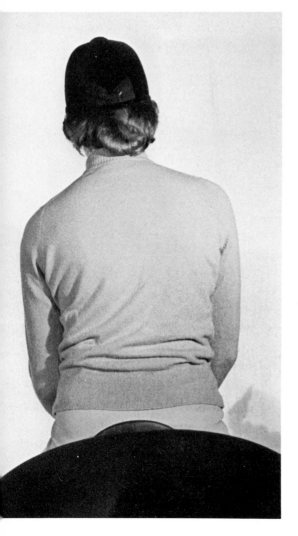

Lateral collapsing of waist.

LATERAL COLLAPSING OF WAIST

Apparent Fault
Unless the rider is collapsing on one side only (crooked) this fault is really only seen in walk. The rider allows his body to rock from side to side as well as backwards and forwards. His shoulders sway and his upper body tips first to one side and then the other. This is a bad fault which has simply become a habit, as it encourages the horse towards a two-time walk. It frequently accompanies unequal rein contact: one hand going back as the other comes forward.

Cause

First one side of the rider's waist, and then the other, collapses above the hip. He therefore does not experience the sustained feeling of remaining equally balanced on his seat bones.

Correction

The rider must be aware of the weight on his seat bones and not allow it to transfer from one to the other. He must sit 'tall', with the feeling of having a piece of string attached to the centre of his head drawing him upwards. He must lift his rib cage upwards, lengthening the area between the sternum, where his ribs join at the front, and the waistband of his breeches. By being conscious *only* of the tilting forwards and back of his pelvis and spine he should be able to eliminate his unattractive movement. Once a rider realises that he does this it is usually not too difficult to eradicate the fault.

Recommended Exercises

Spine Mobility (1), (2) and *(4)*.

ROUND SHOULDERS AND BOWED HEAD

Apparent Fault

The rider with rounded shoulders and a hanging head really just has an extension of the 'collapsed waist' problem. It can, however, be due to a physical deformity born of bad posture, often called 'The Dowager's Hump'.

Cause

Weak upper back and neck muscles.
Bad habits.

Correction

As for *Collapsed Waist*. General posture must be improved. The rider must realise that constantly looking down will probably result in a confirmed posture problem. He must also realise that the horse can feel the smallest movement of his head, as it makes up a seventh of his total body weight.

Recommended Exercises

Spine Mobility (1), (2) and *(4)*.

'The Dowager's Hump': a collapsed spine in the area of the shoulder blades.

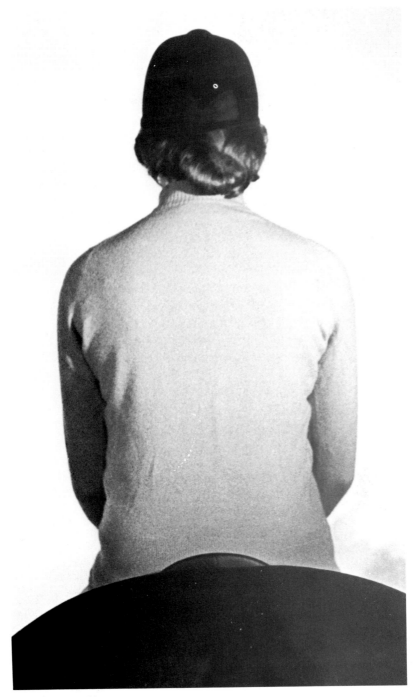

Round shoulders.

THE INEFFECTIVE LEG

Apparent Fault
The rider's heel is often raised above his toe and the whole leg looks weak and limp. The knee comes 'up' the saddle. The rider is inclined to 'kick' instead of applying a subtle aid. Whatever he does with his leg is rather ineffective.

Cause
The rider is not putting any weight into the stirrup or heel. Because of this, his calf muscles are flabby and soft, so his leg aid is rather flabby and imprecise.

Correction
The weight must be allowed to flow down into the stirrup iron, and via the ball of the foot to the heel. There must be a balance between the two. The rider must think of bringing his knee a little further under his hip and 'growing downwards'. The foot should take the weight of the leg in all sitting paces and the weight of the rider's body in rising trot.

Care should be taken not to put too much weight in the heel, or the lower leg may go too far forwards. Conversely, if the rider's lower leg comes too far back, more weight in the heel will help to correct it.

The heel should be down, with the weight equally spread between it and the ball of the foot.

Recommended Exercises
Ankle Exercises (1) and (2).

ANKLES ROLLED UNDER

Apparent Fault
The rider's leg is 'wrapped round' the horse so well that he actually bends the joint, holding the foot against the horse's belly.

Cause
The rider is not spreading the weight correctly across his stirrup iron. He has too much on the outside edge so that his little toe tends to be much lower than his big toe.

Correction

Keep the ankle joint straight, feeling the weight equally across the whole of the ball of the foot.

Remember that if the ankle is in any way crooked the tension in the joint will stop it acting as a shock absorber.

Recommended Exercise

Ankle Exercise (1).

The ankle incorrectly rolled over in an attempt to bring the leg against the horse's side.

LOOSE KNEE

Apparent Fault
The rider's knee hangs away from the saddle and the back of his calf comes against the horse's side. Obviously his toe hangs outwards as well.

Cause
The rider is turning his leg out from the hip joint. This can also happen with a fat-thighed rider whose flesh is a contributing factor.

Correction
If flesh is the problem, drawing the fat and muscle back from between the saddle and the thigh bone can help, but it is generally muscle tone that is lacking, and a conscious effort must be made to keep the leg softly against the saddle. This is achieved not by closing the knees but by turning them inwards from the hip joint. Sometimes a short-legged rider on a fat horse

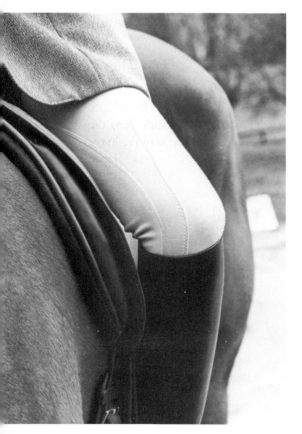

A loose knee.

can be excused this fault for it is the only way he can get his lower leg anywhere near the horse's sides.

Recommended Exercises
Hip Mobility Exercises (1), (2), (3), (4), (5) and (6).
Legs and Feet (1), (2) and (3).

DROOPING HANDS

Apparent Fault
The rider's hands are held below the line of elbow-hand-horse's mouth, yet they are not stiff. In fact they are probably quite the opposite and rather limp.

Sometimes the fingers are 'open' as well.

Cause
The rider is not 'carrying' the weight of his own hands: instead he is letting them weigh downwards towards a resting place on the horse's neck.

Correction
The fingers must be closed round the reins without being clenched into fists. The rider must then support the weight of his own hands using the upper arm muscles, rather than the lower arm muscles. Use of the lower arm muscles often makes the rider's hands bounce up and down; so-called 'dancing hands' are generally attributed to the use of these muscles.

Sometimes it is helpful to imagine that you are carrying two cups of tea with saucers, which is about the weight of a human hand. Be ready to hand the cups of tea forward.

Recommended Exercises
Shoulder and Arm Exercises.

OPEN FINGERS

Apparent Fault
The rider holds the reins in the tips of the fingers. The hand is not properly closed.

151

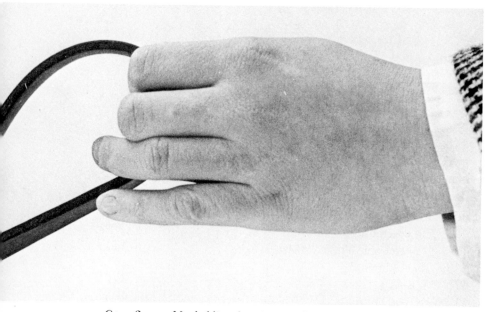

Open fingers. Not holding the rein securely is a common fault.

Cause

The rider's hand is only half holding the reins and he is not offering the horse a secure enough rein contact. He probably misguidedly thinks that he has 'light hands'. Open fingers are a weak and ineffective way of riding, and the rider is far less sensitive to the movements of the horse's head than when holding the reins correctly.

Correction

The rider must close his fingers properly round the reins without clenching his hands. See *Chapter 13*. Being aware of holding the hands up and not letting them droop is sometimes helpful.

Recommended Exercises

Finger Exercises.
Shoulder and Arm Exercises.

CHAPTER

21

When the brain gets in the way

Having covered most of the obvious rider faults I am left realising that there still are some left which cannot be categorised. These belong to the mind or the brain.

Although it is the 'reflex' action which generally helps our day-to-day self-preservation, in riding it often seems to get in the way. When something startles a horse and he therefore becomes more afraid, we tighten; or when he bucks we clutch with our legs, instead of relaxing and taking the weight in our stirrups.

One of these 'mental' problems relates to unequal hands. We continue to contort our arm positions even when we know perfectly well that we are doing the wrong thing; crossing one hand over the neck is the perfect example. It will never stop a horse falling in on a circle, yet most riders find that when faced with this difficulty it is their first line of defence. Lifting the outside hand up and over the neck when the horse falls out on to its outside shoulder is another of these odd reflexes.

It seems to be in our nature to oppose with our hands the direction which the horse wishes to take. We have, you might say, become too 'handy'. We try to 'push' him back with the reins. The only cure is really to get it fixed in our minds that the horse does not necessarily go in the direction in which he bends his neck. He does go, however, where his legs go. This is the part that we as riders must concentrate on controlling. The horse's body is controlled with our body and legs: *not* with our hands.

Our eyes are partially to blame for these problems, as unfortunately we tend to bow our heads and focus closely on the head and neck in front of us, mesmerising ourselves into thinking of nothing else.

Our brain is entirely responsible for these and similar problems such as holding our breath. They have nothing to do with physical difficulties and can only be overcome when the rider can free himself from the bondage of his brain and eyes. He must seek and find not only physical balance but also mental equilibrium and tranquility.

Once the rider has achieved physical balance he is free to begin to discover the great art of horsemanship. He is now ready to learn the subtleties of communicating with a horse through knowledge and understanding, and for this he will need a calm mind.

To achieve the ultimate goal psychological and physiological balance must work together in a perfect partnership.

INDEX

Aids, riding 10, 37
  application of 61-3, 67
  back 77-82
  body 62
  hands 62, 68-76
  legs 62, 64-7
  rein 68-76
  seat 62, 77-82
  voice 62-3
  weight 77-82
Ankles
  elasticity of 37, 55
  exercises 89, 132
  rolled under 148-9
    apparent fault 148
    cause 148
    correction 149
    recommended exercise 149
  stiff 131-2
Antagonistics (muscles) 38, 93, 121-2
Arms
  drooping 75
  exercises 89-90
    lungeing 93
  at halt 34, 37-8
  'heavy' 34
  length of 16, 18
  loose 94
  stiffness of shoulders and 134
  weak 59
Automatic responses 153-4

Back
  aids 77-82
  bracing the 79
  in canter 52-3
  effect on, of incorrect seat 30
  exercises 86-7
  in forward seat 53-5
  at halt 33, 34
  hollowing (concave) 78-9
  rounded 54
  rounding (convex) 78-9
  in sitting trot 49
  suppleness of 15
  tension of hip and 123-4
    apparent fault 123
    cause 123
    correction 124
    recommended exercises 124
Balance
  in canter 53
  exercises for 85-6
  faults relating to 96-108
  lack of 56-60

loss of 69
and lungeing 92-3
physical and mental 154
in saddle 7, 8, 32-9, 80
sense of 24
and top heaviness 15
in trot 44
Balls of feet
  in rising trot 44-5
Bearing surface of saddle 28
Behind movement (fault)
  in all paces 104-6
    apparent fault 104-5
    cause 105-6
    correction 106
    recommended exercises 106
  in rising trot 96-7
    apparent fault 96
    cause 96
    correction 96
    physical exercises 97
    recommended exercise 96-7
Bit, discomfort of 62
Blindfold,
  riding 22
  test for feel 21, 69-71
Body
  aids 62
  v. brain learning ratio 11-12
  ideal shape for rider 14-19
  structure 41
Bouncing hands 135
  apparent fault 135
  cause 135
  correction 135
  recommended exercises 135
Bracing the back 77-9
Brain
  v. body learning ratio 11-12
  'getting in the way' 153-4
Breasts, over-balancing due to
    large 15
Breathing
  exercises for rider 90
  of horse 24
Bridle 68, 92
Bumping 71, 79

Calming horse 62
Calves, gripping with backs of 128-30
Canter 40, 51-5
  faults in 102-3
  twisting in 116-17
Centred Riding (Swift) 97
Centre of gravity 32, 34, 44

inability to find 93, 96
Chair seat (sitting too far back in saddle)
    106-7
    apparent fault 107
    cause 106
    correction 106-7
Chest, and turning 82
Circles 82
    lungeing 92-3
Clutching tendency, combatting, 56-8, 60,
    94
Collapsed hip 109-11
    apparent fault 109-10
    cause 110
    correction 111
    recommended exercises 111
Collapsed seat 101-2
    apparent fault 101
    cause 101-2
    correction 102
    recommended exercises 102
Collapsed spine 145-6
Collapsed waist 143
    cause 143
    correction 143
    fault 143
    lateral 144-5
    recommended exercises 143
Collecting influence 79, 80
Communication between horse and rider
    59, 62-3, 154
Concave (hollowing) back 78-9
    concentration on self, as valuable to
        novice 19
Conformation of horse and rider 14, 36-7
Contact of lower leg 64-7, 94
Contraction of muscles 38, 93, 121
Convex (rounding) back 78-9
    excessive 54
Correcting
    faults 19-20
    one thing at a time 19
Correct position
    faults in 95-152
        re balance 96-108
        re crookedness 109-20
        re tension 121-41
        re looseness 142-52
    fundamental problems of 56-60
    at halt 32-9
    importance of 7-9, 10, 77
Counter-canter 51-2
Crookedness
    of rider's physique 20, 85
        faults relating to 109-120
    of stirrup 133
        apparent fault 133
        cause 133
        correction 133

Deep seat 93
Diagonals, changing 46-7
Dialogue, instructor-pupil 12
Discomfort 12
Double bounce in rising trot 97-8
    apparent fault 97

cause 97
    correction 97
    recommended exercises 98
Double bridle 68
'Dowager's Hump, The' 145-6
Dressage horse
    competitions 62
    physique of typical rider 14, 15
    saddle 26, 91
Drooping
    of arms 75
    of hands 151
        apparent fault 151
        cause 151
        correction 151
        recommended exercises 151

Ears, at halt 33
Elasticity 83
    of ankles 37-55
Elbows
    in canter 53
    exercises 89
    at halt 38
    held out 135-7
        apparent fault 135
        cause 137
        correction 137
        recommended exercises 137
    in walk 41-2
Exercises for rider 83-90
    ankles 89
    arms 89-90
    balancing 85-6
    breathing 90
    fingers 89
    on ground 85-90
    hip mobility 87-8
    legs and feet 88
    lungeing 93-4
    for rider position faults 96-152 *passim*
    shoulders 89-90
    spine mobility 86-7
    see also recommended exercises *under*
        specific faults
Eyes
    focussing of 21, 153-4
    looking forward 94

Fatness of rider 17
Faults, rider position 95-152
    re balance 96-108
    re crookedness 109-20
        additional 119-20
    caused by looseness 142-52
    caused by tension 121-41
Feed back 73
Feel, sense of 21-2, 52, 57, 69
Feet of rider 18
    exercises 88
    at halt 37
    right home in stirrup 134
        apparent fault 134
        cause 134
        correction 134
Fence, approaching 55

Fingers
  exercises 89
  open 151-2
    v. closed 38
  squeezing 74
Fitness of rider 16
Fixators, muscles as 121-2
Flap, saddle 27
Floppiness, problems of 60
Fork seat 100-1
  apparent fault 100
  cause 100-1
  correction 101
  recommended exercises 101
Forward
  driving influence 79-80
  seat 53-5

Gallop 40
Gentle precision 37
Grinding teeth of horse 24
Gripping
  with backs of calves 128-30
    apparent fault 128
    cause 128-9
    correction 129-30
    recommended exercises 130
  with knees 127-8
    apparent fault 127
    cause 127-8
    correction 128
    recommended exercises 128
  upwards 119, 120
Ground exercises 85-90
  ankles 89
  balancing 85-6
  fingers 89
  hip mobility 87-8
  legs and feet 88
  shoulders and arms 89-90
  spine mobility 86-7

Halt, correct position at 32-9
Hands
  aids 62
  bouncing 135
  drooping 151
  exercises 89
  in forward seat 54
  at halt 37-8
  position of rider's 16
  and rein 69-76
  unequal positions of 119, 153
  in walk 41
Hanging exercises 86
Harmonisation with horse's movements 94, 154
Head of horse, movement of
  in canter 53
  in walk 41
Head of rider
  at halt 33
  held crookedly 119
  in sitting trot 50
  upright 94
  wobbling 60

Hearing, sense of 22-4
Heaviness
  of arms 34
  of shoulders 15, 94
Heels
  at halt 33, 37, 38
  in rising trot 45
  too low 130-1
    apparent fault 130
    cause 130-1
    correction 131
    recommended exercises 131
Hip 14
  in canter 52-3
  collapsed 109-11
  and exercise 83-4, 87-8
  in forward seat 54
  at halt 33-4, 35, 38
  joint
    and hip bone 32
    importance of in riding 83-4
  in light (modified) seat 55
  mobility 87-8, 94
  one in advance of the other 111-12
  in rising trot 44-6
  -and-shoulder configuration, in turning 82
  in sitting trot 48-9
  suppleness of 35
  tension of back and 123-4
  in walk 40-2
Hollowing (concave) back 78-9

Ideal physique of rider 14-17
Ineffective leg 148
  apparent fault 148
  cause 148
  correction 148
  recommended exercises 148
In front of movement (fault)
  in all paces 102-4
    apparent fault 102-3
    cause 103
    correction 103-4
    recommended exercises 104
  in rising trot 98-9
    apparent fault 98
    cause 98
    correction 99
    physical exercises 99
    recommended exercises 99
Injury of rider
  inhibiting body function 20
'Inside' of movement, in turning 81-2
Instruction, need for constant 13
Instructors
  choosing 10-12
  and lungeing 91-3
  roles and functions of 11
    in checking faults 95
Involuntary movements 7

Jensen, Anne-Grethe 15
Joints 57
Jumping 40
  saddle 26

Knees, of rider
in canter 53
correct position of 94
in forward seat 54
gripping with 127-8
at halt 34, 35
in light (modified) seat 55
loose 150-1
in rising trot 44
in walk 41

Lateral collapsing of waist 144-5
apparent fault 144
cause 145
correction 145
recommended exercises 145
Leaning
forward 58-9
inwards 81
Learning 10-13, 19, 80
Leg(s), of rider
aids 62, 65-7
in canter 53
exercises 85, 88
at halt 35-6
ideal shapes 14-15
ineffective 148
position of 64-7
problematic shapes 18-19
in walk 41
weight of 64-5
Ligaments, suppleness of 39, 83
Light (or modified) seat 55
Listening 23
Long-leggedness
advantage of 66
disadvantages of excessive 66
of dressage-horse rider 14
Long-thighed rider 46
Looseness
correct amount of 94
faults caused by 142-52
of knee 150-1
apparent fault 150
cause 150
correction 150-1
recommended exercises 151
problems of 60, 142
Lower leg 18
in canter 53
contact of 64-7, 94
exercises 88
at halt 37
position 64-7
too far back 104
apparent fault 104
cause 104
correction 104
recommended exercises 104
in walk 41
Lungeing 9, 91-4
exercises 94, 99
gear 91-2
horses 91
Lungs 90

Marzog 15
Mental problems 153-4
Modified (or light) seat 55
Movement, unnecessary 140-1
Muscle(s)
development of 17, 38
and exercise 83-4
functioning of 39, 121
lack of tone 19, 20, 60, 83
loosening 56-8
losing 38
tension and relaxation 121-41
tight seat 124-5

Narrow saddles 27-8
Neck
at halt 34
stiff 139-40
Novice riders 7, 19, 52, 64
problems for 56-60

One hip in advance of the other 111-12
apparent fault 111-12
cause 112
correction 112
recommended exercises 112
One shoulder dropped 113-14
apparent fault 113
cause 113
correction 114
recommended exercises 114
Open fingers 151-2
apparent fault 151
cause 152
correction 152
recommended exercises 152
Overall tension 122
apparent fault 122
cause 122
correction 122
recommended exercises 122
Over-instruction 134

Pain of rider
dealing with 20
Pelvis
and saddle 27-9, 31
in sitting trot 49
structure of 41
in walk 40
Physical defects of rider 20
Physique of rider 14-20
ideal 14-17
problematic 17-19
Point of balance 45, 56
Praising horse 62
Prime movers (muscles) 38, 93, 121-2
Pubic bone, angle of and saddle 27
Punishment of horse 24
'Pushing' 77
in walk 41

Racehorse
physique of typical rider of 14
Rein
aids 62, 68-76

at halt 37-8
  holding 68-71
  tension 72-3
  weight 71-2
  width 68-9
Relaxation and tension 121-41
  muscular 121-2
  and overall tension 122
  of seat muscles 94
Rhythm
  of horse
    listening to 22-4
    in canter 51-2
    in trot 43
  of rider's breathing 90
Rider(s)
  novice 7, 19, 52
  physique of 14-20
  position faults 95-152
  varied ability of 11
Rigidity 59-60
  and exercise 83
    lungeing 93
Rising
  crookedly 114-16
    apparent fault 114
    cause 114
    correction 116
    recommended exercises 116
  too high 108
    apparent fault/cause 108
    correction/exercise 108
  trot 43-7, 92, 108, 114-16
    behind movement in 96-7
    double bounce in 97-8
    in front of movement in 98-9
Rounded shoulders and bowed head 145,
  147
  apparent fault 145
  cause 145
  correction 145
  recommended exercises 145
Rounding (convex) back 54, 78-9
  excessive 54

Saddle
  hunting *v.* dressage 26
  ideal 26-7
  importance and influence of 26-31
  rising too high in 108
  sitting too far back in *see* chair seat
Scolding horse 62
Seat bones
  aids 62, 77-82
  balancing on 32, 33, 34
  in canter 53
  faults in position 100-2
  in forward seat 54
  in light (modified) seat 55
  relaxation of 94
  in rising trot 43-7
  and saddle 27
  in sitting trot 47-50
  tight muscles 124-5
  in walk 40
Senses of rider 21-5

Sensitivity of horse
  to aids 61
  to rider's loss of balance 58-9
Sheath noise 24
Short-leggedness
  and choice of saddle 27
  problems of 18, 67
  and rising trot 46
Shortness of racehorse rider 14
Shoulders
  in canter 53
  exercises 89-90
  at halt 33, 34, 38
  heavy 94
    overbalancing due to 15
  -and-hip configuration, in turning 82
  one dropped 113-14
  round 145, 147
  stiffness of arms and 134-5
  in walk 40-2
Sight, sense of 21
Sitting
  and riding 15
  too far back in saddle *see* chair seat
  trot 47-50
    faults in 102
  see also correct position
Slack, in rein 72
Slimness of rider 14-15
Smell, sense of 24
Sounds of horse, listening to 22-4
Spine of rider 16, 20
  in canter 52
  in light (modified) seat 55
  mobility of 78-9, 94
    exercises for 86-7
  in rising trot 44
  in sitting trot 48
  in walk 40-2
Steps of horse, in walk 40
Stiff ankles 131-2
  apparent fault 131
  cause 131-2
  correction 132
  recommended exercises 132
Stiff horse 117-18
  apparent fault 117
  cause 117
  correction 117
  recommended exercises 117
Stiff neck 139-40
  apparent fault 139
  cause 139
  correction 139
  recommended exercises 140
Stiffness *see also* rigidity
Stiff shoulders and arms 134-5
  apparent fault 134
  cause 134
  correction 134-5
  recommended exercises 135
Stiff wrists 137-8
  apparent fault 137
  cause 138
  correction 138
  recommended exercises 138

see also rigidity
Stillness of legs, re horse's body 64-7, 94
Stirrup(s)
　crooked 133
　foot right home in 134
　shortening for forward seat 54
　working without 92-3
Straightness *see* upright posture
Submissiveness 8
Suppleness 14, 15, 35, 39, 53, 64, 83, 94
　over-, problems of 60
Swift, Sally 97

'Tall in the saddle' 81
Teeth of horse, grinding 24
Tendons
　suppleness of 39, 84
　'tense' 57
Tension
　back and hip 123-4
　faults caused by 121-41
　of jaw 140
　　apparent fault 140
　　cause 140
　　correction 140
　　recommended exercise 140
　and looseness 142
　and muscle function 121-2
　overall 122
　of rein 72-3
　of rider 56-9
　　lungeing to banish 93
Thighs 14, 18, 19
　exercises 88
　in forward seat 54
　at halt 34, 35
　length and flap of saddle 27
　in light (modified) seat 55
　in rising trot 44, 46
　tight 126-7
　in walk 41
Tightness
　of seat muscles 124-5
　　apparent fault 124
　　cause 124
　　correction 124-5
　　recommended exercises 125
　of thighs 126-7
　　apparent fault 126
　　cause 126
　　correction 126
　　recommended exercises 126-7
Toes
　correct position of 94
　turned out 132-3

apparent fault 132
cause 132
correction 132
recommended exercises 133
Top heaviness 17, 18
Touch, sense of 22
Tree (frame of saddle) 27
Trot 40, 43-50
　rising 43-7
　sitting 47-50
Turning 80-2
Twisting in canter 116-17
　apparent fault 116
　cause 116
　correction 116-17
　recommended exercises 117

Unequal hand positions 119, 153
Unnecessary movement 140-1
　apparent fault 140
　cause 141
　correction 141
　recommended exercises 141
Upper body of rider 14-15, 17
　in canter 52
　in rising trot 44-5
Upright posture 15-16, 32-3, 47-8, 54, 55,
　81, 94

Voice
　aids 62-3
　rider's use of 24-5
　tone of 62-3

Waist
　in canter 52
Walk (equestrian) 40-2, 92
　faults in 102
Walking (human) and riding 15
Weak-armed rider 59
Weight 92
　aids 77
　of rein 71-2
　of rider's leg 64-5
Width
　of rein 68-9
　of saddle 27-8
Wobbling head 60
Wrist
　bending, and rein 75-6
　stiffness of 38, 137-8

Yoga and riding 84, 122
Young, untrained horses 62